The Prepared Life

Guidebook for Successful Living in the Power of the Holy Spirit!

By C. S. Lovett

Edited and Illustrated by L. Lovett

ABOUT THE AUTHOR

Dr. Lovett was the founder of Personal Christianity, a fundamental, evangelical non-denominational ministry. For 61 years, he had but one objective—preparing Christians for the second coming of Christ! This book is one of over 45 of his works designed to help believers be prepared for His appearing.

Dr. Lovett's decision to serve the Lord resulted in the loss of a sizable, personal fortune. He was well equipped for the job the Lord had given him. A graduate of American Baptist Seminary of the West, he held the M.A. and D.Div. degrees conferred *Magna Cum Laude.* He also completed graduate work in psychology at Los Angeles State College and held a Ph.D. in counseling from the Louisiana Christian University.

He was a retired Air Force pilot/instructor/chaplain (Lt. Colonel) and was married to Marjorie in 1942 until he "graduated to glory" in 2012. He leaves behind two daughters, two grandchildren and two great grandchildren.

For more information about C. S. Lovett and his ministry, please contact www.cslovettbooks.com, email us at info@cslovettbooks.com or you may write to:

Personal Christianity
PO Box 918
Middleton, ID 83644

CONTENTS

INTRODUCTION

Are You Prepared?

"No eye has seen, no ear has heard, and no mind has imagined what God has prepared for those who love Him" (1 Corinthians 2:9).

That verse tells us God has already prepared a "wealth of spirit" beyond imagining for those who love Him, and all we need to do is prepare ourselves to receive it.

Right now you have a tremendous opportunity you can't afford to miss. The prepared life is an abundant lifestyle. The process of growth and change into the likeness of Christ is exciting. The power of Christ's Spirit working through you is absolutely thrilling! You know who you are, why you are here, and where you are going. Not only will you be prepared to deal with today's problems and end-time events, you will also be ready for the future with an outstanding place at Jesus' side in the kingdom.

Why You Need to Prepare

The last days are upon us. Current events are quickly setting up for end-time prophecies to be fulfilled. Israel is the country to watch for the first sign that the seven-year tribulation will soon begin. Israel is totally surrounded by enemies. The middle-east is in turmoil, racing to get nuclear weapons, and determined to wipe Israel off the map. In America and other countries, God is replaced with gold, immorality is king, and lawlessness is queen. America, Israel's main supporter, is soon to collapse both morally and fiscally, leaving Israel to fend for itself. Christians will once again be persecuted for their faith. Unsuspecting Christians will be caught off-guard and not know how to cope with the satanic onslaught.

How to Prepare

No matter what stage you are in life, you can have the power to (1) overcome the problems of today's world, (2) be steadfast in all you do so you can fulfill your purpose in life, (3) be secure in your faith, (4) be able to withstand all the devil's onslaughts, and (5) be totally prepared to meet the Lord.

This book is your guide for victorious living under any circumstance. The first part is about the gifts God gives us at salvation, including the Holy Spirit. Then there are chapters about the Spirit, who He is, and what He does; and then how to find your special gift. The rest of the book focuses on four directions of your life with specific "Spirit power actions" that enable the Spirit to work through you.

With each step, you will notice many positive changes the Holy Spirit is bringing about in your life, and you will be increasingly prepared for your ministry. Go as far as you are able and God will be pleased. Being close to the Lord and seeing the

Spirit's power guiding you in your daily life is more wonderful than words can describe!

Let's get started!

LIGHT ETERNAL

One

AT HOME IN THE KINGDOM OF HEAVEN

"Blessed be the God and Father of our Lord Jesus Christ, who has blessed us with every spiritual blessing in the heavenly places in Christ" (Ephesians 1:3).

Mysteries Revealed in the Bible

People are God's passion, spanning all ages and races! God's Word is a telescope through which we

11

see far beyond ourselves, both back to before the beginning and forward past time and space into eternity. In the Bible the great mysteries of God are revealed and the created finds the Creator. Through the Bible, we come to know the eternal Triune God—Father, Son Jesus Christ, and Holy Spirit—living within every believer. We know who we are, why we are here, and where we are going. We are all equal in His eyes and He has no favorites. Whosoever will may come and receive all the promises God has to offer.

What Is Heaven?

A simple definition is that heaven is a place where God dwells, and the place prepared by the Creator for His children to be in union with Him forever. Why do we think about it, write songs about it, and let our imaginations soar as we gaze into the nighttime sky attempting to find it among the stars and the far reaches of space? It's because heaven is a great mystery to us, full of wonder and speculation. But it's far more glorious than a simple definition could ever describe.

Heaven Is a Christian's Real Home

So where exactly is it? Actually there are two heavens mentioned in the Bible: the first one is the temporal **physical realm** above the earth, namely referred to as sky, atmosphere, or universe in Genesis, Psalms and many other places.

The second one is neither sky, nor anything above the atmosphere, nor anywhere in the vast reaches of the physical universe. This heaven is not physical at all, but in an entirely different realm. It is in the invisible **spiritual realm** called **eternity.** The eternal spiritual realm is the **real** world, because it always existed apart from space and time. It is our **real** heaven and home, where the eternal Godhead (Trinity) dwells with all His holy angels, and where Christians go to be with the Lord forever after their bodies die.

The great mystery is that the everlasting spiritual heaven exists **alongside** the physical heaven and universe which are part of space and time.

Your soul (also called mind, "image of God," and spirit) is **eternal**, and it was created for the spiritual heaven, but your body cannot sense it. Your physical body was created exclusively for your time on earth. Each one of us has to spend eternity someplace—either heaven or hell—and on earth is when we choose where to spend it. When a Christian's body dies, it is shed as the spirit takes flight to God's eternal kingdom and you are able to see it in all its glory. Everyone else spends eternity in a spiritual realm called hell with the devil and his angels.

Glimpse of Heaven through the Son

For now, God has intentionally kept His unseen spiritual heaven mostly hidden from us. We live by faith, not by sight. He wants to be loved for who He is, not for what He can give us—and does not want to influence our choice of which god we will serve.

However, we are not kept in the dark. Until Jesus revealed mysteries about the Kingdom of Heaven, God was known as the Almighty Yahweh of the Old Testament to be feared, revered and never seen. At His coming, the Son revealed the true nature of His Father. He called God, "My Father," and in His language was a life of intimacy and open access with the Father. God is the essence of love and compassion, and gave the promise that His true believers would become His children and share in the kingdom of the Father and Son in heaven.

The Secret Kingdom

For about three and a half years on earth, the Son of God revealed many things about the heavenly kingdom. Jesus called heaven the Kingdom of God, Kingdom of Heaven, and Paradise. He spoke in code (parables) about it frequently. He came to found a kingdom, not a school; and to initiate a relationship, not a religious system. He came to reveal the Father's love for His children and restore the open fellowship with the Creator that Adam and Eve had severed long ago by disobedience in the Garden of Eden.

Jesus' Sermon on the Mount (Matthew Chapters 5-7) was not a mere ethical code, but its sublime moral principles far surpassed all human moral standards.

His universal eternal principles laid out the basis for the kingdom for all time. He revealed the supreme purpose in life—and how to achieve it!

He taught us how to pray at the Sermon on the Mount, beginning with, *"Our Father Who is in heaven..."* (Matthew 6:9). No one even dared to think of Yahweh as Father. But Jesus said He is our loving Father as well. Then He continued, *"Look at the birds of the air: they neither sow nor reap nor gather into barns, and yet your Heavenly Father feeds them. Are you not of more value than they?"* (Matthew 6:26). Children of such a Heavenly Father are extremely valuable to God.

Teaching in Code

The Savior could never publicly say, "I am the Messiah," or He would have been immediately taken into custody. He could not openly proclaim himself Messiah-King or reveal the secrets of the Kingdom of Heaven to everyone. He walked a magnificent fine line of successfully teaching the principles of God's kingdom while keeping the rulers from killing Him before His mission was completed.

He was able to do this by speaking in the code of parables, allegories, metaphors, and illustrations; and often began a story with "The Kingdom of God is like..." The story would be easily understood and interpreted by believers, but mysterious to rulers and other nonbelievers.

The greatest thing He revealed was that the *"Kingdom of Heaven is within you"* (Luke 17:21). It is not physical at all. **It is private, inward and spiritual.** *"To you it has been granted to know the secrets of the Kingdom of Heaven, but not to them"* (Matthew 13:11). With the Holy Spirit's indwelling, believers have the kingdom and all its privileges within them now. The Spirit enables His insiders to see the secrets (mysteries) of the kingdom that were previously hidden from the prophets. The basic secret common to all kingdom parables is this: in Jesus, God's rule (kingdom) has come to human experience in a **new spiritual form.**

Jesus' Preparation for Our Heavenly Home

At the Last Supper, Jesus prepared His disciples for His departure, giving them a vision of His heavenly home where they would eventually join Him. Christ's words in the following verse are among the most beautiful descriptions of heaven, *"In My Father's house are many dwelling places; if it were not so, I would have told you; for I go to prepare a place for you. If I go and prepare a place for you, I will come again and receive you to Myself, that where I am, there you may be also"* (John 14:2-3).

Since our Lord tells us that heaven is a place of many homes of which we can scarcely imagine how wonderful they will be, Jesus is even now preparing these homes for His people! That may seem impossible to us, but that's what He said. To remove our doubts, He added for emphasis, *"If it were not so, I would have told you."* The Master Carpenter who was born into an earthly home is well prepared for building our heavenly homes.

No Greater Love

By submitting to death, our Lord took away its power for all time by burying its shaft into His own heart. He bore the weight of every sin that every one of us has ever committed, and endured every moment of every sinner's isolation. He who was utterly sinless endured the torment of the damned, the conviction of being eternally separated from God that is called the Second Death. No man could have endured this. Only Almighty God could have endured it. Having given His life as a ransom with His precious blood, He obtained eternal redemption and life for all humankind. There is no greater love than this!

Both Jesus' death and resurrection were necessary to complete the redemption of humankind and open the door to heaven. A dead Christ might have been a teacher, wonder worker, and a sacrifice for sin; but only a risen and living Christ could be the Savior, the Life, and eternal life giver! The advent of God in human form was so earthshaking that it split the calendar into B.C. and A.D.!

Who can understand this kind of love, or even fathom its meaning? Praise God we don't have to, but only accept it on our knees in great humility. We love

Him, not because He can give us everything we want, but because He gave Himself to us, even though He had to sacrifice His only begotten Son on a cross in order to do it. We have Him as our Father, and we are destined to live in His house forever.

Christ's Spirit at Home in Us

When the Day of Pentecost arrived A.D. 30, all believers were immediately freed from the law of sin and death, and endowed with eternal life. With Christ's own sinless nature in the form of the Holy Spirit dwelling in them, there was a tremendous change in the form of salvation and worship. The God of the New Testament was a loving Father, and worship was now internal in spirit and truth (John 4:23-24). From that moment on, their true reality was the spirit world, God the ultimate reality, and heaven their eternal destination.

The Old Testament form of salvation and worship was erased. People were no longer required to be a Jew by birth or conversion to Judaism to be saved. No more animal sacrifices for sin, or Jewish leaders telling them what to do with unbearable rules and regulations added to the Law of Moses. There was no longer any need for Temple worship because believers' bodies are the Temple of the Holy Spirit (1 Corinthians 3:16). Only the human body can house Christ's Spirit, and God is accessed directly through the Spirit.

Mystery of Christ in You

"I (Paul) became a servant to put God's word into full effect: that secret purpose hidden for long ages and through many generations, but now disclosed to God's people. To them He chose to make known this secret purpose: Christ in you" (Colossians 1:25-27).

The mystery of "Christ in you" is the miracle of the new birth of the Spirit with Christ's own righteous nature. Since the Godhead is a Trinity, the Holy Spirit is also referred to as the "Spirit of Christ." This is one of the great themes of the New Testament.

We are "stamped with the seal of the Holy Spirit." It is our spiritual genetic code. It becomes a permanent non-physical part of our being, not tangible in any way. But it is as real as our physical DNA genetic code given by our Creator. Our current physical genetic code is subject to flaws, mutations, and death; but our spiritual genetic code is perfect, pure, and gives eternal life.

Only God's spiritual genetic code unlocks the secrets of the Kingdom of God and allows us to enter heaven. It also allows us to understand our Creator's magnificent plan hidden from the beginning of time. As His children, we are blessed beyond measure. Present redemption is only a foretaste of what eternity holds, and the presence of

His Spirit in our hearts is like a deposit, guaranteeing our inheritance and all that is to come. We cannot be unborn or aborted.

In heaven, we will live in perfect fellowship with God our Father. We will be at home with Him as His children, and all the privileges of living in His family will be ours; we will live in the light of His eternal love.

These magnificent truths are just some of the secrets of the kingdom. It is much better to know heaven is going to be a pleasant surprise. Knowing what it is really like would be too wonderful to bear and even understand. God's plan for us is to take Him at His word, and by faith believe that what He has in store for us is beyond our wildest dreams—and we will love it! We will never be bored, we will love whatever God asks us to do, and it will be perfectly suited to our gifts.

Now you are ready to enter into the privileges of the kingdom and power the Holy Spirit has to give!

"To go to heaven, fully to enjoy God, is infinitely better than the most pleasant accommodations here." —Jonathan Edwards

WORD OF GOD

Two

GOD'S GREAT GIFT

"…but the free gift of God is eternal life in Christ Jesus our Lord" (Romans 6:23b).

God's Awesome Salvation Privileges are a GIFT

They have to be! They are too precious and priceless to be bought or sold, and they can never be earned. That's why they are a free gift to all who believe. The Lord has done great things for us because He loves us; the Cross is proof of that. But all are things we could never do for ourselves. Salvation is free but after that, everything else is earned. Anything we can do, He expects us to do. That's our part.

Our salvation privileges are so rich and full that it is impossible to list everything we have in Christ, but I am listing the most essential items. First, I will show what it does include; then later by contrast, I can show what it does not include, and what your part is. Here are seven specifics of salvation you need to know:

1. Eternal Life. This comes as a free gift of God. But what do we receive exactly? A substance added to our souls which makes it possible for us to live forever? No. It has nothing to do with longevity. Every soul (also called "spirit" or "image of God") is designed to live forever someplace. That comes with being created in God's image. Bodies, of course, were not designed for eternity. Nothing physical is eternal. God does not have to add anything to our souls to extend human existence.

After we are born, our souls exist eternally now, and after our bodies die, they keep on existing whether in heaven or hell. We were put here on earth to decide of our own free wills where we will spend eternity, and with which god — Jesus in heaven or Satan in hell.

More precisely in the New Testament, eternal life is a union with God now and in heaven after the body dies. A person joined to God at salvation receives the gift of eternal life. Those in heaven will know the blessedness of union with God; those in hell will know the agony of eternal union with Satan (called the Second Death).

We know little about life in the spirit world, but we can be sure this union (eternal life) brings completion. That is what our souls ache for. Perhaps the closest thing which approximates it is marital intimacy. In heaven, we will enjoy something not possible on earth—total intimacy. Our souls will be satisfied by Christ. Earthly intimacy is but a shadow, and the body only gets in the way. Surely the intimacy of spirit-to-spirit will surpass anything we can know body-to-body. Apostle Paul pictured it as a profound mystery of Christ and the Church: "I have betrothed you to Christ."

2. Sonship. Paul says, *"The Spirit you received brought about your adoption to sonship. And by Him we cry, 'Abba, Father'"* (Romans 8:15). He also says, *"Therefore if anyone is in Christ, he is a new creature"* (2 Corinthians 5:17). When we are saved, we become sons and daughters of God by birth. There no human process which can accomplish this. The Seed which produces our spiritual birth comes from above. A spiritual conception occurs which is not religious theory, but a new creation. It is by this means that we acquire the divine nature. The second (new) birth is fathered by the Holy Spirit.

3. Holy Spirit. At salvation, the Holy Spirit comes (is given) to indwell every believer. He performs a number of functions: (1) He serves as a seal, legally securing God's property. (2) He is a down payment in kind, providing even now a sample of the presence of God we will know in heaven. (3) He witnesses to our own spirits that we belong to God. (4) He certifies truth so that we are not dependent on men to validate what is of God. (5) His power makes it possible for us to live a holy life, and for us to perform our tasks and use our gifts as servants of the Lord. (6) He unites all true believers into one body, the church. (7) He coaches and prompts Christians to press toward maturity in Christ. The Spirit, Himself, is a gift. (See also Chapter 3.)

4. Righteousness. The instant we are saved, we are clothed with a robe of righteousness. This is the new nature. It was typified by Israel's high priest and his glorious robe. Within such a robe (new nature), sinners can be comfortable in the presence of a holy God. Obviously such a robe cannot be produced by sinful people. It was produced by the sinless Son of God and given to us at salvation. By this, He did for us what no human can do for himself. Since this robe is real, it cannot come by way of a decree from any religious group or body. It is not theological, but actual. We literally partake of the divine nature.

The Christian has two kinds of righteousness. At salvation, he is provided with the robe which grants him instantaneous righteousness. It is given to us by

Christ upon receipt of the new nature (robe). However, inside that robe, the person himself is expected to advance into the likeness of the Lord. The personal righteousness of an individual is developed as enabled by the Holy Spirit. It is important to separate these two kinds.

5. Forgiveness. For example, say I owe you five dollars. I don't pay. You elect to forgive my debt. Who pays? You do. Your five dollars are gone. The one who forgives, pays. If we are forgiven the guilt of our sin, someone still must pay the penalty. Jesus did. He took upon himself the total guilt of all sin. He paid the penalty for all sin. Forgiveness comes to us as we personally confess our sin and receive forgiveness as individuals. Confession is something we do. The act of forgiving is something God does. Jesus has already paid the penalty, and the Word says "He is faithful" to forgive us.

6. Authority. When we receive Christ, we receive a commission or calling. We are expected to use our talents as servants of the Lord. God delegates responsibility and also grants us the authority to carry it out. Our salvation privileges include the right to speak to people in the Name of the Lord. His Spirit backs our words so that people accept our authority and respond to the truth.

This authority extends to citizens of the spirit world as well as the physical world. Since the work assigned to God's servant meets with satanic opposition, authority over Satan must be included within the commission. Christian work is crippled, if not futile, without the exercise of this authority. The devil has a wile which clouds the truth of our authority over him. It is the "safe in Christ" wile, which suggests there is automatic armor for Christians. Of course there is not because Paul told us to put it on. The moment one begins to use this authority, the truth of James 4:7 becomes operative: *"Resist the devil and he will flee from you."*

7. Inheritance. The Lord Jesus has an inheritance coming. He invites us to share it as "joint-heirs." For Jesus to inherit from His Father, means He does so in the role of "Son." What does Jesus inherit? The Kingdom! This is why He says, *"Come, you who are blessed by My Father; take your inheritance, the kingdom prepared for you…"* (Matthew 25:34). That is our invitation. We receive it when we are saved. Therefore, we expect to see the Lord in His kingdom. He even instructed us to pray for it, *"Your kingdom come…"* (Matthew 6:10). The kingdom features the appearance of Jesus, once more on earth and reigning in glory. We are to share this with Him. As joint-heirs of this kingdom, we will also be revealed with Him, covered with His glory. Every Christian will participate in this whether he is alive at the coming of Christ or not. Those who have died in Christ, God will "bring with Him."

Our Rewards Are EARNED

"I press on toward the goal for the prize of the upward call of God in Christ Jesus" (Philippians 3:14).

With Christ's Holy Spirit within us, we have the power to earn our rewards. The gift of the salvation privileges is what God does toward us. Earned rewards are what we do toward God. Notice the difference in directions.

God's blessings come down to us; our responses go up to God. Anything we can give God is not part of our salvation privileges. Granted, the ability to serve Him comes via the Holy Spirit, but meeting our responsibility isn't. The indwelling Spirit enables us to fulfill our obligation to God, but His presence does not relieve us of our responsibility to live a productive life. To the contrary, we have even less excuse for faithlessness. The Lord gives us the opportunity, and our part is taking advantage of it to the maximum of our abilities. We are to stay in the race and keep running toward the finish line until we cross it in victory. This is what pleases God. He wants His children to win at life.

"Well Done, Good and Faithful Servant!"

Jesus' "Parable of the Talents" (Matthew 25:14-30) shows the necessity of using well what God has entrusted to us.

"It will be like a man going on a journey who called his servants and entrusted his property to them. To one he gave five talents of money, to another two talents and to another one talent, each according to his ability. (A talent was worth more than a thousand dollars.) Then he went on his

journey. The man who had received the five talents went at once and put his money to work and gained five more. So also, the one with the two talents gained two more. But the man who had received the one talent went off, dug a hole in the ground and hid his master's money.

"After a long time the master of those servants returned and settled accounts with them. The man who had received the five talents brought the other five. 'Master,' he said, 'you entrusted me with five talents. See, I have gained five more.'

"His master replied, 'Well done, good and faithful servant! You have been faithful with a few things; I will put you in charge of many things. Come and share your master's happiness!'

"The man with the two talents also came. 'Master,' he said, 'you entrusted me with two talents; see, I have gained two more.'

"His master replied, 'Well done, good and faithful servant! You have been faithful with a few things; I will put you in charge of many things. Come and share your master's happiness!'" (verses 14-23).

The last man with the one talent hid it instead of investing it. When he came to the master with no return on his investment, he was severely punished. The lazy disobedient servant was bankrupt in his spirit, and his one talent was taken away and given to the man with the ten talents. Those who bear no fruit for God's kingdom cannot expect to be treated the same as those who are faithful. We must not make excuses to avoid doing what God calls us to do. If God truly is our Master, we must obey willingly. Our time, abilities, and money aren't ours in the first place—we are caretakers, not owners.

Talents represent any kind of resource we are given. God gives us time, gifts, and other resources according to our abilities, and He expects us to invest them wisely until He returns. We are responsible to use well what God has given us. The issue is not how much we have, but how well we use what we have. The master divided the money (talents) among his servants according to their abilities, without regard for the opportunities given to other Christians. No one received more or less than he could handle. If he failed in his assignment, his excuse could not be that he was overwhelmed.

The person who diligently invests his or her time and talent to serve God will be rewarded. Faithfulness to the task—even though opportunities differ—brings exactly the same reward. Each of us is rewarded based only on what we do and not what someone else does. We can all be faithful with what we have, and this is all the Master requires.

Enter into Your Reward

"Behold, I am coming soon and I am bringing with Me My reward to compensate everyone according to what he has done. I am the Alpha and Omega, the First and the Last, the Beginning and the End. Blessed are those who

wash their robes so that they may have the right to enter the city by the gates and eat from the Tree of Life" (Revelation 22:12-14 Lovett's Lights).

Jesus' return will be like lightning flashing across the sky. As joint-heirs of this kingdom, we will also be revealed with Him, covered with His glory. Every Christian will participate in this whether He is alive at the coming of Christ or not. Those who have died in Christ, God will "bring with Him."

The Lord's first task will be to judge His people and distribute His rewards among them. The rewards are positions in Jesus' government, which will be assigned on the basis of each person's works. The believer will be judged on the basis of what he has done as compared with what he could have done—therefore, competing only against himself. In this way, everyone has an equal opportunity when it comes to winning a good job near Jesus.

This judgment and assignment of jobs will be accomplished before Jesus descends to earth. His government will then be in place and ready to function when the New Jerusalem descends to earth. This should challenge every Christian to put Jesus ahead of fame, fortune, family and fun—and think seriously about his future job in the kingdom.

After the kingdom is set up, we will reign as priests and kings at His side. The most faithful are closest to the Lord's side and receive the top positions. All those temporal sacrifices on earth for eternal wealth of the kingdom have been worth it.

Blood, sweat and tears are replaced with glory, joy, peace, and the presence of God. Wherever He is, we are, never to be separated again. The Age of the Holy Spirit is over and we see Jesus face-to-face and spirit-to-spirit forever.

Keep these concepts in mind:

Where we will be is FREE. Whether in heaven with Jesus or on earth with Him is a matter of a free gift or an inheritance.

What we will do is EARNED. Our future jobs with Christ, whether performed on earth or in heaven are being determined by our faithfulness now.

What we will be like is DEVELOPED. Our persons, i.e., our personalities, are being developed in this life as we react to stresses and strains, testing and trials of everyday life. Every day should find us more like Christ. This is serious perseverance to the end; but if we look to the Lord to help us, we will receive the crown of righteousness.

Soar on Eagles' Wings

"Do you not know? Have you not heard? The Everlasting God, the Lord, the Creator of the ends of the earth does not become weary or tired. His understanding is inscrutable. He gives strength to the weary, and to him who lacks might He increases power. Though youths grow weary and tired, and vigorous young men stumble badly, yet those who wait for the Lord will gain new strength; they will mount up with

wings like eagles, they will run and not get tired, they will walk and not become weary" (Isaiah 40:28-31).

DAY OF PENTECOST

Three

POWER OF THE HOLY SPIRIT

Our Pentecostal Heritage

During His earthly ministry, Jesus taught that His words and works were not His own, but the result of His Father who indwelt Him. The Savior sought to convince His disciples that just as His Father indwelt Him, He would return to indwell them. The Lord insisted that the Holy Spirit could not bring His presence to them until He was glorified. The return of Christ via the Holy Spirit is one of the most delightful mysteries of the New Testament. Apostle Paul develops the truth of Jesus' indwelling. It is by His indwelling that His power becomes ours.

Jesus Prepared His Disciples

Christ's three and a half year earthly ministry was just the beginning of His work. He began something, but as yet He hadn't finished it. His human life was only introductory to a greater work which was not only to be continued, but augmented after His ascension.

During the forty days between His resurrection and ascension into heaven, the Lord gave final instructions to His disciples about the kingdom they represented and how they were commissioned to be witnesses to Christ and spread the Gospel throughout the world. It was a supernatural business, requiring supernatural power. Yet, the Lord assured them they would have everything needed for the job, but it was to come in a strange way. So strange, in fact, their minds could hardly grasp it.

In as much as the work required spiritual power, none of Jesus' disciples could obey the commission until this power was available. As long as Jesus remained in their midst so that His presence was confined to a body, it would be impossible for them to receive the power of which He spoke. It was His plan to return to them via the Holy Spirit and indwell them, empowering them with Himself.

His instructions were: *"I am sending the promise of My Father upon you; but you are to stay in the city until you are clothed with power from on high"* (Luke 24:49).

They did as He asked, waiting in the city of Jerusalem. For nine days nothing happened. Then on the tenth day, the Holy Spirit arrived bringing the presence of Jesus in person! This was the Day of Pentecost, celebrated 50 days after the Feast of Unleavened Bread which was the day after Passover. On that day our inheritance arrived with a bang!

Christ's Return in the Spirit

This is the source of our power! It was swift and unmistakable. Jesus' core group of believers was gathered together in the upper room in Jerusalem. All of a sudden a roaring noise descended out of the sky! It resembled the blast of a violent gale. The sound filled the entire house where they were sitting and shocked them out of their human thoughts and into the spiritual realm. What looked like tongues of fire appeared and began distributing themselves, so that they touched every person present, coming to rest on each one. The believers became aflame with excitement. In that instant they received the "Spirit of Christ" and were "born from above."

There was no doubt about it; Jesus' presence in the form of the Holy Spirit indwelt every believer in the room and they were immediately filled with His power! The Lord was faithful to His promise, *"On that day you will realize that I am in My Father, and you are in Me and I am in you"* (John 14:20). All doubt and uncertainty, all depression and discouragement were swept away instantly.

As a man with a physical body, Jesus could be present only in one place at one time; but as the Holy Spirit, He could be everywhere in every soul that was His own. This magnificent gift of God's presence was to the whole church, and yet to each individual; a precious possession that was to be guarded as an eternal flame within, to be loved and adored.

All that day, word of what happened in the upper room spread through the city. Crowds flocked to hear Peter and the others fearlessly give testimony to the death and resurrection of Jesus of Nazareth, without regard for what might happen to them because of their boldness. When this first great day of the Spirit's outpouring in Jerusalem had ended, those who believed what Peter said were baptized and added to the church—about three thousand in all.

Those startling events of the Day of Pentecost changed the congregation of believers as nothing else could have done. There was no turning back, no doubt about their commission to go forward and preach the Gospel in the power and authority of Christ's Spirit to as many who would listen. The 120 disciples who gathered in the upper room that night knew God was so close they could feel His hand upon them.

Power of Pentecost

The Day of Pentecost began a new era. The New Covenant (Testament) was now in effect and the Age of the Holy Spirit had begun!

The church was born that day, and the Lord has been adding members ever since. From the moment of the Spirit's arrival in the world to empower believers, right up to this second, Christians have the privilege of serving Christ in that same power. Pentecostal power started that day and it hasn't ceased. It is still available to those serious about the Master's command. As long as the Great Commission is in force, the power to carry it out is available.

Greater Works

In the days of His flesh, Jesus did many miraculous works. Again and again He pointed to them as evidence that the Father was in Him. Then, at the Last Supper, He promised the apostles:

"I tell you the truth, anyone who has faith in Me will do what I have been doing. He will do even greater things than these, because I am going to the Father." That is, when He returned to Spirit since "God is Spirit" (John 4:24).

Once out of the flesh and back in the Spirit, He could commence His work as the Great Baptizer, the *"One who baptizes in the Holy Spirit"* (John 1:33). Notice that He did not say "lesser works" but "greater works." And how are we to do them?

"And I will do whatever you ask in My name, so that the Son may bring glory to the Father" (John 14:12-13.

In other words, we are to do these greater works by asking Him to do them through us. We are just carrying them out in His name and in His will. Every request must fit the plan and will of God, and be in full accord with the righteous character of Christ. The Greek is emphatic about the ego of Christ: "I will do it." Jesus is the One who is going to do it, and He won't do anything contrary to the divine plan or purpose.

New Discoveries of Life in the Spirit

Emancipation from external symbolic religion to internal personal relationship with God was an entirely new experience for Jesus' apostles. Freedom and discovery of life in the Spirit opened up a whole new realm of exploration with limitless boundaries, like our early pioneers of space travel, and they were willing to take risks. They started from scratch and learned by doing as they went along, with only the Holy Spirit to guide them. It was a new, breathtaking and wonderful experience. The disciples now had more power than they even imagined, but had to learn to use it wisely.

The Early Church took Christ at His word and united in prayer as they asked for signs and wonders of healing, until the place was shaken where they were assembled together. Then, people brought the sick into the streets and laid them on beds and couches. Also, a multitude of sick people came from cities around Jerusalem, and everyone was healed. Jesus was there in Spirit as He continued His ministry from the right hand of God through His body, the Church, according to His promise.

Faith of the Early Church

Those early Christians had the Spirit's power and the faith to use it! The Apostles were doing the very thing for which the power of God was promised: obeying their Master's Great Commission, *"You will be My witnesses in Jerusalem, and in all Judea and Samaria, and to the ends of the earth"* (Acts 1:8). The command of the Lord rang in their ears. Nothing could be clearer. When they moved in obedience, the power of God followed. Those early saints seized the privilege of Pentecost and their faith roared into action! By the end of the first century, much of the Roman Empire had heard the good news of Jesus Christ.

What about Today?

Some say, "Oh, that was only Acts and in the beginning of the church, for the purpose of confirming Christ's resurrection. It's 2,000 years later and the gifts have dwindled."

Not true! Only people's faith has dwindled, and therefore their power. Faith is the missing ingredient in our various church bodies and buildings. No faith, no power. All they need to do is rekindle their faith and the power returns. The same Spirit, dwelling in every Christian, is still in effect with all the power of Pentecost until the end of the Age of the Holy Spirit when Christ returns in glory.

The Spirit came to execute for us all the blessings purchased by Christ's redemption and pledged by His redemptive names. Jesus has never lost any of His interest in the work He came to do. If you wish to know how He wants to act today, read how He did act. The book of Acts shows us how He wants to act throughout all the days, even unto the end of the age. Men have named this book "Acts of the Apostles," but it really should be named "Acts of the Holy Spirit."

Works of the Spirit

In addition to what's listed in our salvation privileges in Chapter 2, here are more of the kingdom privileges and power the Holy Spirit gives us:

1. The Spirit **reveals the Trinity** to us. The Holy Trinity is the one God manifested in three personalities —Father, Son, and Holy Spirit. We must not divide the personality of the Godhead so sharply as to divorce the Lord Jesus from the Holy Spirit, since He is called the Spirit of Christ. It was Jesus who returned in Spirit form, and it is in Christ that the personality of the Trinity dwells.

God is the only being that is omnipresent (everywhere at the same time), omnipotent (all powerful), and omniscient (all knowing). There is a single essence to the fundamental nature of God, but He does operate as a Trinity. The Father is also known as the "Creator;" the Son is also known as the "Redeemer;" and the Holy Spirit is the Spirit of Christ/God actively working in the world and through all "born from above" Christians. Since the Holy Trinity is one and the same God, all of God's wonderful names and attributes in the Bible may be used interchangeably. God can manifest Himself in different ways and perform different roles at the same time in every believer's heart.

God is Spirit and has no gender. Gender is an earthly only attribute. Jesus put on a body while He was on earth so we could "see" Him. However, no human can actually see God, for He is Spirit. Right now we worship Him, in Spirit and truth by faith. We will only truly see God when we are in heaven with Him in the spiritual realm.

The main differences of the Trinity are the functions/attributes that allow our spiritually challenged brains to some what understand the Godhead. The "we" and "us" in Genesis 1:26 and 3:22 are our Triune God. The Nicene Creed of the Christian Church spells it out well, and this is what separates true Christians from religious cults (see Appendix).

2. The Holy Spirit's confirmation with our spirits that we are the children of God and joint heirs to the kingdom gives us **direct access to the Godhead** (Trinity) at any time. This is awesome! There is no

need of a priest or any other intercessor. Christ is our only intercessor to God. His Spirit is a holy seal, certifying that we are His children and rightful heirs.

3. Our bodies are the **temple of Christ's Spirit** who resides in us. We are able to hear His "still small voice" which guides and protects our lives.

4. The Spirit gives **insight** into all things in both physical and spiritual realms, gives us discernment so we can judge the worth of anything, and confirms what is true.

5. He revels the **meaning of God's Word** (the Bible), and the things prepared for us that are beyond our seeing, hearing, and imagining.

6. The Spirit comes to the aid of our weakness, gives us **power** for healing and miracles; power to resist evil thoughts and desires, and overcome Satan, temptation and sin; and power to live righteous lives.

7. The Spirit gives each of us our own unique set of **gifts** (talents) and purpose for our lives, activating our gifts as we move in His power.

8. When we don't know how or what to pray, the Spirit understands our inarticulate groans and **intercedes** for us in accordance with God's will.

9. **Fruits** of the Spirit are: love, joy, peace, patience, kindness, goodness, faithfulness, gentleness, and self control.

10. The Spirit **unites** all believers in love.

Access His Power Today

If the same Spirit which brought our Lord Jesus from the dead dwells within us, are we to remain calm about it? To the contrary, access to the power of God multiplies the drama of being alive! Operating in the supernatural power of God's Spirit is the most awesome adventure a human can know. Those first century saints knew it. They lived in the thrill of Christ.

The closer you draw to Christ and move in His power, the more miracles you will see. Expect the supernatural. This is part of the exciting privilege of Pentecost and the power to execute the Great Commission.

Seeing the Supernatural

Remember Jesus' first recorded miracle? He was at a wedding feast at Cana in Galilee when an embarrassing situation developed. The host ran out of wine. The situation was so awkward that the Lord's mother came to Him about it. From His words she sensed He would take care of it, so she gave orders to the servants, *"Whatever He says to you, do it"* (John 2:5).

Standing nearby were six stone water jars, each holding 20 to 30 gallons. The Lord commanded the servants to fill the jars to the brim with water and take a sample to the banquet master. Somewhere in the process, the water became wine. When the banquet master tasted the most excellent wine, he had no idea where it came from. Then the Holy Spirit adds the exciting answer, *"but the servants knew"* (John 2:9).

But how did the servants know? They knew because they were working closely with Jesus. They were intimately involved in what He was doing and saw the supernatural. This is true today. The Lord is still doing miracles in our time. Not just miracles of healing, but the way He opens doors for us, creates opportunities for us, touches hearts to change lives, bears witness to our words when we speak for Him, and even gives us unexpected things that delight us. I'm sure you can think of more. All this is supernatural. If we work with Him at close range, we get to see the supernatural. And when we do, it keeps our hearts aflame.

Confirm Your Salvation

Take a moment to make sure you have the source of God's power. Being a Christian is not any form of external religion. It is not belonging to a church or movement. It's not even knowing that Jesus is God. Even the devil knows this.

A Christian is a "new creation" in Christ, and this is totally different from all other religions. An actual spiritual transformation takes place—a new birth in your soul with Christ's Holy Spirit. Some call it the "born again" or "born from above" experience. The Spirit becomes a permanent non-physical part of your being, not tangible in any way, and you have an internal personal relationship with God. People must be born from above to get God's Holy Spirit. The necessity is absolute and is universally binding.

Anyone, even the worst sinner, can become a "new creation" in Christ and receive the Holy Spirit! But it is not automatic. God will not violate a person's free will. One must want Christ to come into his life. When he does, all he has to do is open his heart to Jesus and ask Him into his life. Instantly the barrier to God is gone! This individual is born from above with God's Holy Spirit, and he becomes a totally new person. Any person can be cleansed from sin and start over fresh. Our loving Savior invites anyone to become a part of His family, enter the Kingdom of God, and share in the eternal wealth of spirit He has promised to all who believe.

Be still for a moment and you'll sense an inner invitation to open it as He speaks those words to you personally, *"Here I stand at the door and knock. If you hear Me calling and open the door, I will come in…"* (Revelation 3:20). You have a free will to choose where you want to spend eternity, and with whom; and the Lord won't violate it. He humbly seeks permission to enter your life, bringing complete forgiveness for your sins and the gift of eternal life.

In the same way you'd open the door of your home to a friend's knock, you can open your heart to Jesus. Say something like this to Him in prayer, "Lord, please forgive me for all my sins. Thank You for dying for me so that I may have Your gift of eternal life. I open the door of my heart and invite You to come in. Reveal Your presence to me. I want You for my Savior and Lord."

He will come in, and you will instantly be born from above with the indwelling of His Holy Spirit. The peace you feel is proof of His presence. This is just the beginning of blessing. You will have a personal relationship with God, be empowered to accomplish your calling on earth, live an abundant life that is pleasing to the Lord, and experience eternal life and joy, totally secure in the family of God—forever!

In Christ, all people are treated equally. There is no racial barrier, gender barrier, or social barrier. Whoever has faith to obey God, believe in His Son, and receive His Holy Spirit shares in all the promises and blessings of the salvation package and the Holy Spirit of God!

Get Involved with the Spirit of God

Receiving the Holy Spirit is a spectacular beginning. Getting acquainted with Him provides added astonishment.

The amount of power in a Christian's life is directly proportional to his activity with the Spirit of God. Paul calls it "fellowship of the Spirit." It is one thing for a person to appreciate the knowledge of sins forgiven, quite another to experience the realization of supernatural power. A Christian will not find himself with the wonder of Christ until he daily uses his privileges of power.

Those who study the Bible to learn of the Holy Spirit have a treat coming when they meet those truths in action. They are so different when they happen to you. It is one thing to store the knowledge of the Spirit, quite another to experience Him in your soul. Many of you who read these lines already know how glorious it is to experience the presence of the Holy Spirit. What you may not know is that beyond that experience is another—the thrill of moving in His power. That experience is so exciting it leads you to the desire of obeying the Lord. All the pleasure, excitement and delight we can hold beckons from the Great Commission.

- The hallmark of a Christian is **power!**
- The excitement of a Christian is the **wonder** of working in that power!
- The privilege of a Christian is the **thrill** of moving in that power!

PATH OF PEACE

Four

YOUR SPIRITUAL GIFT AND LIFE PLAN

"But to each one of us grace was given according to the measure of Christ's gift" (Ephesians 4:7).

This chapter is about what spiritual gifts are and finding yours. This is very important, because knowing enables you to set up a life plan, set goals to use your talents to the fullest, and be great at what you do. The Spirit gives us the gift, guidance and power, but the rest is up to us to fulfill our calling. We have tremendous freedom to accomplish our life's work.

The Creative Gift

We live in a wonderful world—a world revealed to us through our senses, but at the same time far more than what our five senses alone can recognize. Because we are created in the image of God, we can spiritually "see" love, the beauty of a landscape, or the noble act of helping someone without thought of personal gain. We know when someone has great faith, even though we cannot perceive it with our eyes. Scientifically speaking, these things do not belong to the physical senses, yet they are part of our daily experience.

To co-create with God is our human destiny. Creativity is a way of life, no matter what our talents are or how we earn our living. Our creative gifts are endless, as God is endless! God gives us inspiration to express ourselves in infinite forms of talents and creative thinking. When we do, we are at the same time praising Him.

A person in the very act of creation is working in complete and total faith. Nothing is impossible! The work has a reality beyond the person's vision. If he is the servant of the work and allows the Holy Spirit to use it for the glory of God, then it becomes greater than the actual work. This is the purpose of our gift! We can live creatively with God's help;

building our lives on Christ, the foundation of our faith, with the talents we have been given.

We Have a Splendid Heritage of Empowered Gifts

The Apostle Paul said, *"We are God's handiwork, created in Christ Jesus for the life of good deeds which God designed for us. Each of us has been given a special gift, a particular share in the bounty of Christ. How vast are the resources of His power open to us who have faith"* (Ephesians 2:10).

Sometimes God chooses the most peculiar people to be vessels of genius because He looks at their hearts and sees, not what they are, but what they could be. The men and women to whom Jesus gave this gift were ordinary human beings, faulted and flawed like the rest of us. He did not disqualify Mary Magdalene because she had been afflicted with seven demons; or Matthew because he was a Jewish tax collector for the Roman government. God did not spend a lot of time looking for the most qualified people, the most adult. Instead, He chose people whose only qualification was childlike faith. Even though the Master gave His disciples no job descriptions, except to preach the Gospel to the world, He knew they had gifts perfectly suited for their calling.

When Christ returned in the Spirit on the Day of Pentecost, the Holy Spirit empowered all believers to put their talents to use for the glory of God.

Every Person Has a Gift

The gifts of God are not limited to the church or reserved for outstanding believers, but are given to every Christian. Even the lowliest Christian has some spiritual gift. God's power is displayed in such a way that it is clear the Spirit is working through that person. The one true God accomplishes His will in different lives by working in different ways so each of us can fulfill our calling.

Regain the excitement of the early church now! The same Spirit and same gifts are just as alive today as they were then. Many of us have just forgotten that we have them and how to use them. And there are so many more that are unique to every individual for use in today's world. All that's needed is a willing heart.

"You have to live the life you were meant to live." —Peggy Wood, from *The Sound of Music*

Ready to Live Your Life to the Fullest?

Have you found your true calling? Are you ready to do what you've always wanted to do? Are you willing to work with the Holy Spirit to accomplish your goals?

You can do it all with the power of the Holy Spirit backing you! Remember, every person has a talent or ability for use in today's world. There is no such thing as a non-gifted believer. Our talents are needed now more than ever. Much work is left to be done in these last days at every level of expertise, flashy or not. We are only required to develop our individual gifts to the fullest of our abilities. It's what we do with what we have been given. All gifts have the same value, none more important than others. All are done for the glory of God—whether serving in church or out in the world serving people.

"Now there are varieties of gifts, but the same Spirit. And there are varieties of ministries, and the same Lord. There are varieties of effects, but the same God who works all things in all persons" (1 Corinthians 12:4-6).

Find Your Talent and Start Winning at Life

"If you can't figure out your purpose, figure out your passion. For your passion will lead you right into your purpose." –Bishop T. D. Jakes

Ask yourself the following questions and then answer honestly. Do you remember when you were young and the world was new and wondrous, and you saw everything through a child's eyes, wanting to touch, feel and explore it? Did you find something you really enjoyed, were good at it, and wished you could do it for the rest of your life? Did you follow that dream, develop your talent, and use it to help people? Or did you do the practical thing in order to please someone else, or because you thought it was the only way to make a living?

Already Know Your Gift?

If you are passionate about what you do, feel you are in God's will for your life, love what you do, are satisfied you are doing great work and would do it even if you never got paid, then you have already found your special gift.

Don't Know What It Is?

If you do not know your gift, or you're not happy with what you are doing, ask God to reveal your purpose in life and what your gift is. His answer will be something for which you are ideally suited—and you will love doing it. Usually, it is something you already have an interest in and wished you could do. Or it may be something entirely different with a talent you didn't even know you have, and you will be pleasantly surprised when it is revealed to you.

And when it is revealed, be great at it! This is your true calling and something only you can do in a wondrous way. Remember, we ourselves do nothing. It is the Holy Spirit who accomplishes all through us. The best stuff comes through you, not from you.

The Lord also knows your personal desire for success in what you undertake in the world and ability to enjoy the good things in life. Spiritual and personal success is what God wants for you too, and He wants you to prosper in both. You should always strive to be the best in all you say and do in the power of the Holy Spirit. The Lord gives us His best, and it should be that way with you. This is your gift to God.

God's Life Plan for You

"Success for the Christian is to find the will of God —and then do it." –Pastor Charles E. Blair

When you know your gift, it's time to set goals. If you can dream it, you can do it. Let your spirit soar and your mind wander.

If you are just starting your life's work, in the middle of it, or even retired, you can change your lifestyle to maximize your high calling in Christ. When your motives are right, the Holy Spirit is eager to give you the power that enables you to accomplish your work and fulfill your dreams. Anything seemingly impossible becomes possible. Your Heavenly Father knows your godly goals concerning what you'd like to accomplish for yourself, others, and the Kingdom of God. He's pleased that you want to use your gifts to the fullest.

Here are the steps:

1. Set feasible goals. When you list them, your mind immediately begins to program your brain to take action, and your creative energies concentrate on achieving them. While you think and pray, the Lord may suddenly give you an idea. When your body is at rest, your mind becomes active and inspiration flows like water. Have pen and paper or electronic notebook handy.

2 . Research your goals. What are you willing to put into pursuit of them? The right choices are important.

Are you willing to make any and all changes to fulfill your calling?

It may be necessary to develop a particular talent or skill through training and discipline; or sometimes the gift is just given with no training needed. It's up to you to know the difference and develop your abilities to the utmost. Techniques must be learned and practiced until they are as perfect as you can make them. Only then are you free to let go and let the Spirit guide you. The crucial thing is to keep your eyes focused on Christ and your goal. You are tremendously free, for you have God's form on which to build your freedom; you know who you are, where your talent comes from, and that you and your talent will live forever.

3. People are spiritual treasures. Find those who are successful at what you want to do. If they can succeed, so can you. Ask questions. Learn what works, and most importantly, what doesn't work. They'll know that answer too. Acquire the skills necessary to be successful. Go to school, take classes, go to your local library or do whatever it takes to be knowledgeable and confident enough to make informed decisions. There may be many resources specifically on making a living with your chosen career. Surf the internet and read all you can.

If you believe in yourself and are excited about your goals, others will be too. It is amazing how far enthusiasm will go when you want to share your gift. Others will want to help you and give you their money and support. Don't be reluctant to accept help. That may be their calling.

4. Create a financial success plan. It is impossible to see and work effectively, but getting organized is necessary and simple. No one builds a house without blueprints (or computer aided design) and a financial success plan (budget). These two things are also your key to success. They enable you to define your vision and achieve your goals. They show everyone you are serious and passionate about fulfilling your dream. Even if money is not an issue, it is still necessary to know where you are going and how to get there. Proper planning is essential. It's your roadmap to success.

5. List your goals in order of priority. All successful people have a feasible plan of action to use their time and money wisely. Your plan needs steps for how to implement it. Get input from family and friends, especially when the plan involves other family members. Make sure everyone is of the same mind and it accommodates their goals as well. You may or may not be in a position to do anything yet, but when you have your plan of action, decision-making is easy.

Decision-making basics: Get all the facts, weigh both sides, ask the Holy Spirit for wisdom, sleep on it, and don't go overboard. You do what fits into your goals, and eliminate what is not part of your plan. It's that simple! With God's help and guidance, many things that seem to be impossible are suddenly doable.

"Run in such a way as to get the prize" (1 Corinthians 9:24b).

6. Go for it! Put your plan into action! If necessary, take baby steps, do one thing at a time, and even a gradual change over a lifetime will eventually get you to the finish line. It's amazing how focused energy, rightly applied, can accomplish your goal, and how less effort goes to unimportant things. Do something and help someone each day. Have faith in your abilities. God goes into action when you are serious, and sets up things in their proper time, always giving you more than you ask for— or even imagine. The simple steps in this chapter will put you on the road to success. It's never too late! (See Matt. 20:1-16, Parable of Workers in the Vineyard.)

"What we go through as we move toward our God-given goals is perfectly planned to make great people capable of handling a great dream." —Lloyd John Ogilvie, from the book *Lord of the Impossible*

SPIRIT OF GOD

Five

TOTALLY INVOLVED WITH THE SPIRIT

"...let us run with perseverance the race marked out for us" (Hebrews 12:1).

The Christian has one passion—living for the Lord. What makes him that way? He is fully involved with the Spirit. Having tasted God's power, he finds that nothing in this world compares with it. The world has nothing to match the thrills, the excitement, and the adventure of moving in the power of the Holy Spirit.

Maybe you know people who are this passionate about Jesus. If so, you know what I mean. They pour their time, money, talent, strength, and total energies into their task and don't let anything deter them. Paul had that passion, *"that I may know Him and the power of His resurrection"* (Philippians 3:10).

A Christian with the power of the Holy Spirit has that same passion. He has embarked on the adventure of exalting Jesus and it transforms his life. Having tasted the fun, joy, excitement, and heart-pounding delight of exalting Christ in the Spirit's power, nothing less can satisfy him.

Get Personally Involved with Jesus and What He Is Doing!

Remember His comforting promise at the Last Supper, *"In that day (Pentecost) you will know that I am in My Father, and you in Me, and I in you. If you abide in Me, and My words abide in you, ask whatever you wish, and it will be done for you"* (John 14:20; 15:7).

The rest of this book is a detailed plan to help you get totally involved with the Holy Spirit and get the most out of your talents. Remember, the more you develop them, the more the Spirit can use you, and the more miracles you will see. There are four specific courses of action to specific goals—both spiritual and physical. Each chapter has a Spirit Power Action to specific goals.

1. Saviorward

Chapter 6. Passion for God's Presence

Chapter 7. Your Power in Prayer

Chapter 8. The Real Lord's Prayer

2. Satanward

Chapter 9. Blessed Are the Overcomers

3. Selfward

Chapter 10. Don't Worry—Be Happy!

4. Saintward/Sinnerward

Chapter 11. Let Your Light Shine

Chapter 12. People of Power

I recommend you follow the order of the book and set goals for each of the four courses of action. Don't go off in all four directions at once. Pick something that is most urgent and focus on that until you become great at it. Then go on to the next. The order may be determined by your own circumstances, so go ahead and adapt the plan for your own personal use. But please read the entire book so you know all the basics.

The closer you get to the end of each course, you will notice many positive changes the Holy Spirit is bringing about in your life, and you will be increasingly prepared for your ministry. Finish each course using the maximum of your abilities, and God will be pleased. Being close to the Lord and seeing the Spirit's power guiding you to win in your daily life is more wonderful than words can describe!

This is the kind of Christian you could be if serving God became your passion. Your enthusiasm can influence your family and many Christians, rekindling their spirits to reach the people in their own lives. Heart-capturing experiences and adventures will bring them all the delight they can hold. *"If we live by the Spirit, let us also walk by the Spirit"* (Galatians 5:25). When we do, we live in the glow of God's "Well done!"

ALONE WITH HIM, JESUS IN PRAYER

Six

PASSION FOR GOD'S PRESENCE

"You have received a Spirit of adoption, by whom we cry out, 'Abba, Father' " (Romans 8:15).

Jesus Longed for His Father

On many occasions the Savior had to get away and be alone with the Father. Crowds kept pressing around Him to hear Him teach, heal their bodies, and even feed them. He hardly had time to eat or sleep. God's Son longed for the refreshment of being with the one person who knew Him most. Even though He walked in His Father's will and His days were filled with wondrous works, it wasn't enough. Throughout His life on earth, Jesus needed time alone with the Father, and was always in constant communion with Him to satisfy the deepest longing of His soul.

On the night of His arrest, Jesus cried out for reassurance and strength to face His coming hours. Separation from the Father on the cross for our redemption was absolutely the worst agony He could bear; but when the redemption was accomplished, His reunion was divine ecstasy. When Christ arose from the grave, it was overwhelming victory! When He ascended into heaven, He was united with the Father forever. And because of it, we can come to the Father as His children.

Sitting at the Master's Feet

God delights in those who humbly call on His name. He quiets us with His love and welcomes us as true sons and daughters. We are invited to sit at His feet and learn about the Kingdom of Heaven. The real kingdom is one of fellowship and relationship. It was and always will be a personal relationship with our Creator. He rejoices when we choose the one thing worth being concerned about, wanting to be close by His side. If we really know the Father's love, we will relax and rejoice that we are God's beloved, and that everything God has is ours as well.

Love Worth Returning

Anyone who loves as desperately as He does needs to be loved in return. God created us to be family. He delights in doing things for us and wants us to enjoy Him. At the same time, He wants us to realize He has needs, too. He hungers for our fellowship. That's why He created us in the beginning. What God really wants is not furious religious activity done for Him, but time spent with Him. Far from playing hard to get, the Lord is closer to us than our own skin.

"Speak to Him, for He hears, and Spirit with spirit meet. Closer is He than breathing, nearer than hands and feet." —Alfred Lord Tennyson

The Lord wants to be our moment-by-moment companion. He is overjoyed when we involve Him in every part of our lives. Having poured out His love on us without measure, He's thrilled when His children make Him the major part of their daily living. Knowing God personally in this way prepares us to take our place at His side as joint heirs in His eternal kingdom.

Where Our Spirits Meet

Our bodies are "temples of the Holy Spirit," and Christ's Spirit resides in each believer. This is where we meet God. The Lord's Spirit is able to indwell every single heart that will receive Him; and every Christian can have Jesus all to himself. It means we can talk directly with the Lord any time we wish. It thrills Him when we do. He sees everything that goes on in our minds. Nothing is hidden from Him so we can tell Him the deepest longings of our hearts. David had this relationship with God when he wrote this song,

"My heart has heard You say,
  'Come and talk with Me.'
And my heart responds,
  'Lord, I am coming'" (Psalm 27:8).

Where do we talk with Him? A temple must have a sanctuary, a place where God and people meet. In the temple of our bodies, that sanctuary is our imagination. The imagination is the spiritual bridge between the physical body and the Spirit. God is Spirit and so is our imagination (John 4:24). No one can see thoughts.

Here's the secret: By means of the imagination, we can give reality to the unseen Lord. In the Old Testament, the Jerusalem Temple's inner sanctuary was called "the Most Holy Place" (1 Kings 6:16). Only the high priest was allowed to go there once a year to make atonement for sins of all the Jewish people with a sacrifice. Now Jesus is our only High Priest and Intercessor, through His "once for all" sacrifice, and we can boldly come directly to Him and pray—any time and anywhere.

In Matthew 6:6, Christ described it as a room where we are alone secretly praying to the Father.

When we close our eyes to pray, we are immediately in that sanctuary of our imagination. Time alone with God in our "Most Holy Place" satisfies the deepest longings of our souls. Through the eyes of faith we are enabled to give reality to the unseen Lord. Christians should never be afraid to go into their sanctuaries and talk with Him. If we do this regularly, His loneliness will be transformed into feasts of joy.

Since Jesus is the only visible human form of God we know, we can picture Him in a physical body, or worship entirely in the Spirit. We worship, praise, and pray to our Triune God the same way Jesus prayed to the Father. We can worship all three personalities, or focus on one. It doesn't matter because God can manifest Himself in different ways and perform different roles at the same time in every believer's heart. Whatever name or appearance makes the God of the Bible real to us is all that matters.

Come into His Presence

"The instant cure of most of our ills would be to enter the Presence in spiritual experience, to become suddenly aware that we are in God and God is in us." –A. W. Tozer, from the book "The Pursuit of God"

The Savior has been there all the time, no doubt about that. Only now you can see Him in the spirit.

There He is, waiting. See that smile on His face? He knows why you have come. Enjoy that welcome smile as you worship Him. Here are some ways:

1. Love God for Who He Is

Say something like this as you greet Him, "Lord, I love being in Your presence, and that's because I adore You. You're my God! It thrills me to be here. You make me feel wanted and complete. When You hug me and tell me You love me as a father loves his child, you really satisfy my soul. I'm starting to realize you have needs that only your children can fulfill. I want to fellowship with You. Having blessing flow from me to You is new to me. But I'm here to do what I was created to do, bring You all the joy and satisfaction only Your child can give."

As you talk with the Father, being His child and part of the whole family of believers becomes a reality. The more you get to know the Creator, the more comfortable you are in His presence, and the more you know what to say.

2. Worship in Spirit and Truth

"God is Spirit, and those who worship Him must worship in spirit and in truth" (John 4:24).

Woman at Jacob's Well (John 4:7-43)

Just outside the city of Sychar in Samaria was Jacob's Well, named for the land Jacob gave to his son, Joseph.

Jesus and His disciples traveled on foot some thirty-four miles from Jerusalem to reach it. After their arrival, the Lord sent His disciples into town to buy food, while He sat wearily at the edge of the well. He was exhausted; it was mid-day and hot. No one would be expected to come and draw water at this hour, and it was hard work lifting it from over one hundred feet below the surface.

However, someone did show up unknowingly for a divine appointment, a sinful woman who did not want to be detected. After Jesus had told her that He was the living water and then exposing her sinful life, she realized He was no ordinary rabbi. She said, *"Sir, I perceive You are a prophet."* The blackness of her life loomed before her. There was only one thing to do—get right with God.

But which temple was the right one? That was her new concern; her mind was taken up with a place where one goes to get right with God. But there were two places. The Samaritans had their temple in their own country, and the Jews had their temple in Jerusalem. With the Prophet standing before her, she thought perhaps He could give the answer to that age-old question.

Gesturing toward nearby Mt. Gerizim, the sacred hill of the Samaritans, she said, *"Our fathers worshipped on this mountain, but you Jews say Jerusalem is the only place to worship God."*

Aware of what was on her mind, the Lord explained, *"The time is at hand when your worship of the Father will have nothing to do with a specific place, neither here nor at Jerusalem. Genuine worshippers will worship the Father in spirit and in truth; in fact, this is exactly the kind of worshippers the Father wants—even seeks."*

Jesus lead her beyond the controversy of which mountain was the right place of worship. He repeated His profound statement, *"God is Spirit, and those who worship Him must worship in spirit and in truth."* It was the higher worship of a common Father according to His nature; worship neither of Jews nor of Samaritans, but of children. No other way could be acceptable to God. A more Christlike teaching than this could not be uttered. This astounding revelation was not disclosed to His disciples, nor to the rulers of Israel—but to a Samaritan woman with an open heart.

Her faith rose further, *"I know that Messiah is coming, the One called Christ. When He gets here, He will explain all these things to us."* She had come nearer still; she added the Jewish reference to the Messiah and knew He was coming. The woman was really asking, "Are you the Christ?" Her soul responded in spirit; her head didn't grasp it all, but her heart was ready.

He answered her truthfully and clearly, *"I AM who is talking to you."* The sentence sounds a bit awkward in English, but it communicated the sacred "I AM" of Yahweh. This soul cried out, and Jesus answered. Nothing more was needed; she had found her Lord.

Jesus said worship must be in the spirit. Since we worship a Spirit we cannot see, hear, or feel, the worship must be by faith inside the very being of our person. The Most Holy Place in our imagination is the temple of the Holy Spirit. This is the way Jesus prayed to the Father when He was on earth; and we can praise and worship our unseen Lord in the same way.

Worship and praise anywhere. We can worship our unseen Lord in this higher form wherever we are: whether in a church full of people, alone in a secret place, on top of a high mountain, on the seashore, in a garden, or in the desert. We can feel the Spirit's presence in the dead of night or the brightness of day.

All the wonderful names and attributes of our Triune God are there for praise and worship. It thrills the Lord to have you call upon the names of His glorious personalities and attributes. The Old Testament names of God are: I AM and Hebrew consonants *YHWH* (Genesis 4:26), most commonly spelled Yahweh with variations Yeshua, Yehoshua, Jehovah, and Joshua. The New Testament name is Jesus (Greek *Iesoús*) and Christ (Gk. *Christós* "Anointed One") in the four Gospels, Paul's great theological letters of the Trinity and Holy Spirit's work, and ends with the *Book of Revelation's "I am the Alpha and the Omega"* (Revelation 22:13).

We can never run out of names for our marvelous Lord and Savior, and they can't even begin to describe

His wonderful attributes. You'll love Him even more after discovering He really is all those things. His past performances are spectacular: creating and maintaining the world and its laws, creating and caring for His own. And He's still at it, cleansing us daily from our sin and ministering to our needs. His future plans for us far outshine anything we can imagine.

No matter what praise you can bestow on God, it could never be enough. Just open your heart and let it pour out. Praise Him for all the magnificent things He has done. Make up your own words, poems and songs just for God; speak or sing your favorite hymns and poems. You were created for worship, and it comes easily.

3. Listen with Your Heart

Be ready for the Lord's response. This is truly a two-way conversation. When you are in the sanctuary of the soul, talking with Christ, the voice of the Spirit can be quite distinct. At first, you may not be able to hear it, but that "still small voice" is really there communicating with you Spirit-to-spirit. Of course, there is no audible sound, but your spirit picks up the thoughts of what God is saying in the language of the heart. It may take some practice to feel the communication. Even so, it is more like an impression or conviction as thoughts come to your mind. It is a real conversation. One day you will speak face-to-face, but for now you listen by faith. At times, talk is not necessary, just being in Jesus' presence is enough. Close friends enjoy each other without a word passing between them.

As you listen to the Spirit's voice, you may ask God, "What do You want, what are You doing, how do You feel about this, is there anything I can do to help You?" You may be able to comfort the Comforter. Does God need to be comforted? Of course! He gets plenty of hurt, not only by all those who reject Him, but by the neglect of His own children. You can ease His pain. Now you are really ministering to the Lord. He draws great comfort and joy from His child who wants to minister to Him. This blesses His soul beyond description and you feel an outpouring of His Spirit.

4. Include Him in Everything You Do

"The steps of the godly are directed by the Lord. He delights in every detail of their lives" (Psalm 37:23).

This is the story of how Brother Lawrence learned to "practice the presence of God." He was born in Lorraine, a little after 1600, while that area was still part of France. As a young man, although he loved the Lord, it wasn't until he reached middle age that he became serious about a close walk with Him. Lawrence entered a Carmelite monastery in Paris as a lay brother and hoped the monastic life would be a shortcut to his goal. As newest man to enter the monastery, it was his job to scrub the pots and pans after the other brothers had made the mess. It was a detestable assignment and he saw himself as nothing more than a household slave. He hated it. At first, he tried to look at this lowly job as a means of mortifying the flesh, but that didn't work.

Then something happened that changed his attitude and life. In the process of complaining to the Lord about his miserable situation, he began to picture Christ as listening to his gripes. He began to sense the Lord's sympathy. As he continued this practice, God became more and more real to him. Before long he was visualizing the Lord as doing the work with him. With the passing of time, Brother Lawrence and his Lord were laughing about it. The tiresome task became less and less tiresome. Lawrence soon found himself actually looking forward to scrubbing the pots and pans with Jesus. What was once drudgery became feasts of joy. He developed a new obsession—a passion for Jesus' presence. It transformed him! The art of visualizing Christ revolutionized his life.

So intense was his delight in the Lord, his face radiated a glow people could see. Word of his joy spread over Europe to the place where Christian royalty journeyed to see him. They wanted to know his secret, but Lawrence was not a theologian. He just made it his business to know God. There was nothing secret or mysterious about his method. Actually it was very simple. He told them, "We should establish in ourselves a sense of God's presence, continually conversing with Him."

Right now, you can visualize Christ and talk with Him all day long, all night long. You have the Holy Spirit inside you wherever you go, every day, hour and minute. You don't have to be in a home or church; you always have the Most Holy Place in your imagination. Include the Lord in everything you say and do. Even the most mundane chore can be tolerable when you visualize Jesus doing the work beside you. You and the Lord will become very close. It is an awesome way to live in the presence of God.

Spirit Power Action

Take time everyday to worship the Lord in spirit and truth. The most important part of your ministry is a personal relationship with the Lord. Set aside time to fellowship with Him every day or night, and then Christ will be your closest Friend.

"Good morning, Lord!" is a great way to start the day. Then ask, "What would you have me do today?" Then listen for His answer. Inspiration will start flowing, sometimes in buckets. Keep paper and pen handy to catch it. Talk with Him as you have your morning beverage and breakfast, or before, if you eat with family members or friends. Ask God to work in the lives of those close to you and those you meet throughout the day.

The goal is to include Him in everything you say and do. The excitement and adventure is anticipating what the Spirit has in store for you, because you have learned to expect the unexpected —the hallmark of a committed Christian.

Select any of the above ideas to build your relationship and work on that. Then add another when you feel comfortable, and soon you will be in constant fellowship with Christ. In time, you will add your own ideas. When you know Him well, suddenly you will find yourself safely in His presence in whatever situation that may come. When your time comes to leave this earthly realm, you will no longer have to practice His presence by faith; you will really be in His presence, face to face!

"Year after year such Christians are seen to grow more unworldly, more serene, more heavenly minded, more transformed, more like Christ, until even their faces express so much of the beautiful inward divine life; that all who look at them cannot but take knowledge that they live with Jesus, and are abiding in Him." —Hannah Whitall Smith, from the book *The Christian's Secret of a Happy Life*

PRAYER SANCTUARY

Seven

YOUR POWER IN PRAYER

"We can be confident that God will listen to us whenever we ask Him for anything in line with His will; and if we know He is listening when we make our requests, we can be sure that all we ask of Him is ours" (1 John 5:14-15).

This chapter gives practical instruction on how to pray in Jesus' name to produce change and results. Knowing how to pray for God's will and how He works through our prayers will achieve God's best for our lives. We will have a closer walk with Him and be able to help others through our faithfulness in prayer. The more we spend time in prayer, the closer we are to Christ.

When Christians know the mind of the Lord and ask for the right things on His behalf, His words *"I will do whatever you ask in My name"* (John 14:13) will come to pass. The Spirit confirms God's will when each decision is made correctly and gives you peace. Seeking the council of wise and godly Christians also helps with decision-making. Circumstances, sometimes but not always, can dictate wise choices and open doors to go through.

Where to Pray

Jesus' teaching about prayer in His Sermon on the Mount was revolutionary. No one before had taught that God was a loving, caring Father who wanted ordinary people to talk directly to Him. For the disciples to think of themselves in God's presence was a totally new concept.

Christ told them, *"When you pray, you are not to be like the hypocrites who direct their prayers toward people in order to show piety and to be admired for lofty words. I assure you that human praise is all the reward they will get. When you pray, get off by yourself. Go into your secret room and shut yourself up in the presence of God. Then your unseen Father, who meets with you in the secret room, will reward you"* (Matthew 6:5-6).

Secret prayer was just the opposite of Jewish

78

custom. In Jesus' day, the Pharisees loved to stand in the synagogues and public places with great fanfare and display of personal importance. As they lifted their hands toward heaven and recited elaborate prayers to confirm their status with God, they would look out the corners of their eyes to make sure the common people were listening. They really weren't praying to the Lord. They only wanted the praise of the people.

What truly pleases the Lord is to pray in that "Most Holy Place" of our imaginations when no one is watching. Most of the time prayer is a private conversation between us and the Lord. You learned how to do that in the previous chapter, "Passion for God's Presence." It can be scheduled prayer, such as during Bible study; or spontaneous prayer for ministering to the Lord; or to privately help individuals in stressful situations.

Attitude and motive are what count with the Master. There are times when others can hear our prayers, but it should be beneficial to them as well, such as praying for a friend or family member in a home, saying grace at a meal, and praying at a church group or public place. The Lord loves to be included in the normal routine of our lives. We can pray before, during, and after we go through our daily work.

Model for Prayer

Sensing His followers needed help in talking directly to God, Jesus gave them a model prayer.

Believers today have this great privilege, and we all need to fully understand how He wants us to use it. The Lord's Prayer in Matthew 6 shows His followers the difference between reciting prayers and talking to God:

> *"When you start to pray, say something like this:*
> *'Our Father in heaven,*
> *We hallow your name'"* (vs. 9).

It is a beginning phrase to make it easier for believers to talk directly to God as a real person. Jesus told His disciples not to babble meaningless phrases, chant, or repeat volumes of words like the pagans did. They were not to carry on like that, for the Father knew full well what they needed even before they asked.

Still, it is necessary to pray; it accomplishes far more than the mechanics of asking God for something. There are some things the Lord wants Christians to do and the only way they can be accomplished is through prayer. That's why you'll find yourself praying for special projects as the Spirit brings them to mind. Here is the next part:

> *"May Your kingdom come,*
> *May Your will be done on earth,*
> *just as it is in heaven"* (vs. 10).

Prayer is one of the most powerful tools for working with God. We are partners with Christ in this endeavor, and it is essential to have open communication with Him as we prepare for the coming kingdom. His precious children are all He has for this holy calling, and we must pray for His will to be done on earth. Through prayer He reveals His will for our lives, and then through the power of the Holy Spirit we are able to carry it out.

The will of God…

Never contradicts God's Word.

Never leads to extremes.

Never is immoral, unethical or illegal by God's laws.

May lead to hardship, difficulty and suffering; but results may be the most fruitful.

Usually is revealed as you go, and increases your faith.

Always is for your good.

Key principle: When a believer's will goes in the opposite to God's, nothing happens. When a believer's will matches God's, success follows prayer!

Jesus wants us to be specific in our requests and gives examples of what to ask for:

"Give us today our daily bread,
   and forgive us our sins,
      just as we have also forgiven those
         who sin against us" (verses 11-12).

When we pray for our daily bread, we are acknowledging that God is our sustainer and provider. We must trust the Lord daily to provide what He knows we need; but nothing is lowered from the sky, we must earn it and the Lord makes that provision also.

Daily forgiveness is as necessary to the health of the soul as daily bread is for the health of the body. It is impossible to go through a single day without offending God in some way. These sins can come between us and our Creator, disrupting fellowship until we ask His forgiveness. In the same way our Lord forgave us, we should forgive others of sins against us, so there is no lingering resentment in our hearts.

"Please do not allow us to be so tempted
that we are overcome by the evil one.
Help us to overcome him" (vs. 13).

God does not tempt us, but He may allow Satan to tempt us. But even then, never beyond what we are able. Actually, this request has to do with the struggle in the Christian's life, that terrible warfare between good and evil (flesh and spirit). We all need temptation and testing to obtain righteousness. God will not allow untested people in the eternal kingdom. All are involved in a daily battle against sin. The third request is for daily help in overcoming the evil one, sometimes on an hourly basis, or even more than that.

Ask, Seek, Knock

"With all prayer and petition pray at all times in the Spirit" (Ephesians 6:18).

Believers are to pray for answers and results, and do our part in seeking them out. When we come to a door that may lead to good things, we are to take action by knocking and checking out the opportunity. Jesus told us to, *"Be persistent in asking and you'll receive what you're praying for. Be persistent in seeking and you'll find what you're looking for. Keep on knocking and the door will open to you. For everyone who asks persistently, receives; and he who seeks persistently, finds; and to everyone who keeps knocking, the door opens"* (Matthew 7:7-8).

Persistence tells the Savior we trust Him. Each time we make a request we are reinforcing our faith and affirming that God will answer our prayers. Even if the door closes, it doesn't matter. A closed door is just as good as an open one; it still leads to where we should go next. When we investigate all opportunities, Christ will be eager to give us more. So not only do believers have to be persistent in prayer, we have to be persistent in seeking and knocking. Then the right door will open.

Here are other examples of praying in God's will. How can I help bring people into the kingdom? What do you want me to do today? Help me understand the Bible, resist evil, find a needed car, council a friend, use my gift and talents, manage my finances, share my wealth, keep my family safe, provide for our daily needs, help my friends.

Jesus wants to help with every good request — large or small. *"If you, being sinful people, know how to give your children what is good for them, how much more will your Father in heaven give what is good to those who ask Him?"* (Matthew 7:11).

God only gives His children what is best. If we ask for that which is not in our best interests, He won't give it no matter how much we ask, seek and knock. That's really a blessing, even if we don't think so at the time. Usually He has saved us from certain disaster. Later we will thank Him that He didn't grant that request.

Listen for His Answer

We can be sure God always hears every prayer. His timing is always perfect, even though to us He may appear to be catastrophically late. We live in earth's time zone, not heaven's. Other times when we ask for the best things in keeping with His will, we don't get them until we're ready to receive them. The Lord answers prayer in three ways: "Yes," "No," and "Not now."

Reasons why the Master's answer may be "not now:"

1. We have sin in our lives and have lost touch with Him.

2. Something is wrong with our thinking, the request is bad for us.

3. We often ignore the area God wants us to pray and need to refocus our request.

4. We have not done our part in bringing about the answer.

5. He has to wait for us to stop taking matters into our own hands and run ahead of Him with our own ways.

6. We must not get ahead of Him, but wait patiently until the circumstances are set up, and to hold out for God's best.

Thank God No Matter What Happens

Commit the circumstances to God; pray for specific needs as they arise; and be thankful. When you are faithful to thank the Lord for what He is doing, He appreciates that He's not taken for granted and will want to help you more. Not only do you get prayers answered, but at the same time you receive God's peace in the power of the Holy Spirit (Philippians 4:6-7).

Sometimes praying is all you can do when circumstances are out of control. Other things require prayer only, while some things require prayer and action. After you've done your part, the Lord does His part. Through prayer and knowing the Lord's ways, you can see His hand in everything. And what do you say to that?

"For yours is the kingdom and the power and glory forever! Amen" (Matt. 6:13b).

Spirit Power Action

Persistence in prayer is the key to a changed life. Any believer, in any circumstance, can have a prayer ministry. Select a project for the Lord and you to work on together. Whatever is the most urgent prayer for you or for someone else is the best place to start. As long as you are persistently praying in His will, you know you have the Spirit's power in your prayers, and they will be answered. It's an awesome privilege God has given you to use for the benefit of others.

You could possibly be part of a small group that continues the tradition of the early church, where two or three persons gather for the specific purpose of praying together and encouraging one another.

If you want to start a small gathering of your own, you can do it. Even if you have never been in a prayer group and don't know how to start one, it's as simple as inviting friends to dinner—and it includes a feast for the soul. You can have food with the fellowship—even Holy Communion. Pass the word around among friends that on a certain day and time there will be a meeting at your house to talk about forming a prayer group. Don't issue specific invitations so as not to pressure anyone.

When you are together for the first time, discuss what form the group should take. You can begin by simply praying for the Holy Spirit to show you what He wants this fellowship to be. It doesn't matter if people are not very comfortable about praying out loud. That will come with each answered prayer. Their joy cannot be contained in silence.

Your group can decide how often and where to meet. Develop a pattern for the meeting time itself. Possibly a period of quiet, then about an hour's discussion of the study material, and the last fifteen minutes spent in praying together out loud or silently. Accept the discipline of lifting each other up to God every day and of remembering the specific needs each has mentioned that week.

In time, friendship and love will develop that is unbreakable, for we are all travelers together on the journey of faith. Share problems, blessings, defeats, and joys; watch each other grow into a depth of faith that none of you had before. As each prayer is answered, the will of God is implemented, and miracles begin to happen. The power of Pentecost will fill the room, the same way it did over 2,000 years ago in that upper room in Jerusalem!

"The farther I go in prayer, the more mysterious it seems. I can't understand it completely, but I can't explain how electricity works either. I just know from my own experience what happens when I flip on the light switch. So it is with prayer; I know how it works because I have seen it make a difference in my everyday life." —Nancy Peerman, from the book *The Real and Only Life*

ONE IN THE SPIRIT

Eight

THE REAL LORD'S PRAYER

"Not only do I pray for these, but also for those who will put their faith in Me because of their words, that they may all be one. O, that they may be one in Us, even as You Father are in Me and I in You" (John 17:20-21).

Two Lord's Prayers?

Most people are familiar with the Lord's Prayer in Matthew 6, and can even recite it by heart. But did you know there is another Lord's Prayer in Chapter 17 of John's Gospel? What's so special about this one?

Heart of Christ Discourses

At the Last Supper, with the help of the Spirit, John the beloved disciple preserved Christ's last discourses in his memory and kept them safe. The 14th through 17th chapters are called "The Heart of Christ," and to read them for the first time is one of the greatest experiences that can ever come to a person in this world. To read them for the hundredth time is an experience just as great. One can only read kneeling in God's very presence.

Jesus' first and last thought is of the disciples, even though He knows that through the night there will be a scattering before the joy of resurrection morning.

Let's return to that night when Jesus and the Twelve Apostles are secretly gathered in the upper room of a believer's home in Jerusalem (probably parents of John Mark). It is their final time together as they partake in the Passover meal. Christ's arrest is just hours away. During the supper, Judas the betrayer left to do his evil deed.

Now the Savior is free to express His innermost thoughts to the Eleven and prepare them for His return to the Father. He institutes the memorial of Holy Communion, tells them why He must leave, and gives assurance that the Holy Spirit would soon return to indwell each one. While the rest of the city celebrates the Paschal feast, it is a night of sorrow for those in the upper room.

Upper Room Becomes the Most Holy Place

Having opened His heart to the apostles, Jesus now opens His heart to the Father in heaven. At the supreme crisis of the Lord's work, the disciples are allowed to listen and learn the nature of their calling which they are to fulfill.

Now we most reverently enter the upper room and take our place among the apostles. For the first time, we are allowed to listen to what is really the Lord's Prayer; and as we hear, we humbly worship. This great intercessory prayer is the preparation for Christ's agony, cross and resurrection—and outlook on the crown beyond; and reveals His intimate fellowship between the Father and the Son. This is as close as we can get to the secret thoughts and inner workings of the Godhead, and that is why it is so special!

Everything is silent as we wait for the Savior to speak.

Consecration of Our Great High Priest

Jesus raises His head and looks toward heaven as He begins His prayer. The presence and fellowship of the Father become so real that a note of hope, joy and victory ring out, *"Father, the hour has come. Glorify Your Son so that Your Son may glorify You. For You have given Him authority over all humanity. He gives eternal life to all You have given Him. This is eternal life—to know You, the only true God, and Jesus Christ, the One You have sent to earth. I have glorified*

You on earth by finishing the work which You gave Me to do; and now Father, glorify Me in Your presence with the glory We shared before the world began" (John 17:1-5).

The first part of the prayer is the consecration of Jesus as the great High Priest. In praying that the Father would glorify the Son, He is really not asking anything for Himself, but that the Son might glorify the Father. The glorification of the Son—His ministry, death, and resurrection—is really the completion of the work which the Father gave Him to do.

The Son prays not as an inferior asking of a superior, but as an equal expressing His desire to return to the Father, to resume the glory which He laid aside for the incarnation. Then He can fulfill in His disciples the amazing things He has just told them. The cross is part of His glory, for the plans of heaven depend on His sacrificial death. The future glory of God depends on the Pentecostal outpouring of Christ as the Holy Spirit by which the church will be formed and believers gathered into the heavenly family.

Consecration of Apostles

The second part of the prayer is the consecration of the apostles. They immediately realize that they are in the presence of the Son of God who is speaking to the great I AM. Jesus usually went off by Himself to be alone with the Father; they never heard such a prayer as this and dare not move or make a sound. They feel unworthy to be included among the listeners.

In spite of all their shortcomings, words spoken by the Master to His Father are a source of comfort to them, *"I have manifested Your character and personality to the men You gave Me out of the world. They were always Yours, and You gave them to Me because they have kept Your Word. Now they know that everything I presented really has come from You. They believe the message You first gave Me, which I passed on to them. They have accepted it and know with certainty that I came from You, and they now fully believe that You sent Me"* (verses 6-8).

Again His first thought is of those for whose sake He consecrated Himself. These He now solemnly presents to the Father. He is interceding for those whom the Father has specially given Him.

Early in His ministry, our Lord spent a night in prayer before selecting His inner circle of men, seeking assurance that He had those the Father had chosen to give Him. To these, Jesus revealed the Father, and they in turn kept the Word they received. True, they have not yet been enlightened by Pentecost, but they acted on the light they did have. They gazed upon Jesus to behold the personality of God. They testified that He alone had the words of eternal life.

Now they are finally convinced He has come from God because they responded to the inner witness of their hearts. Because of this, the Lord considers them wonderfully victorious, having endured the test. He is therefore pleased to present them to the Father as His own.

Guard Them in Your Name

With infinite tenderness the Savior places His request, *"I am praying only for My disciples. I am not praying for the world, but for those You have given Me, because they belong to You. All that is Mine is Yours, and what is Yours is Mine; and through them My glory is revealed"* (verses 9-10).

"Now I am departing the world; I am leaving them behind as I come to You. Holy Father, guard them in the power of Your name, the name You have given Me, that they may be one, as We are one" (vs. 11).

This is the heart of Jesus' prayer. Knowing what lies ahead for them, He commits His disciples to the safekeeping of the Father. This plea for protection transcends physical harm; their souls are safe in Christ. They are joined in the Spirit to the one body, the invisible church. All Christians are safe in Christ.

On other occasions the Lord did pray for the world, but not this time. Only His disciples merit this kind of safekeeping. The world will of course profit, for the end result is that the world may believe. Since the Word of God is now entrusted to these men, it must also be made secure in them. The world will never have a chance to know God and believe in Christ if these are not preserved. Therefore, this request is limited to His disciples and those who later come out from the world to believe in Him.

"While I was with them, I kept them safe in the power of Your name which You gave Me; and I guarded them so that not one of them was lost, except the one destined to be lost as Scripture foretold" (vs. 12).

The Eleven begin to feel secure and understand Judas' fate. Jesus didn't lose him. Judas lost himself. Christ is satisfied He did everything to save him. In no way does God cause anyone to perish. The prophecy was written in order that Judas' perishing might be evidence of God's foresight, that even the acts of a traitor might be witness to the truth.

His next request asks that the Father would sanctify the disciples in truth, *"And now I am coming to You. I am saying these things while I am still in the world so they may have My joy in full measure. I have delivered Your message to them, and the world hates them because they no longer belong to the world. They are strangers to it, as I am. I am not asking You to take them out of the world, only that You keep them safe from the evil one. As You sent Me into the world, I send them into the world; and for their sake I consecrate Myself, so they may be consecrated by the truth"* (verses 13-17).

As the Father has sent the Son, so did the Son send the disciples into the world—in the same manner and mission. Our Lord awakens the spirit of prayer within His disciples as they watch. They will soon be speaking directly to the Father. The work of God in the world is to be carried on by the apostles and they must not be taken out of it, or even isolated from it. They are to charge into the world with confidence, protected against temptation beyond their powers by the spiritual presence of their indwelling Lord. If they use the Spirit's power, they cannot be defeated.

Consecration of All Believers

Jesus does not pray for the intimate group of disciples around Him alone. With this request, He prays for all who will become believers as the Word of truth passes from the apostles to succeeding generations.

"I pray not only for these disciples, but also for those who put their faith in Me because of their words. O Father, may all of them be one, just as You and I are one; as You are in Me and I am in You, so also may they be in Us, and the world will believe You sent Me."

"The glory which You gave Me I have given to them. In order that the world may know You loved them as You loved Me, I pray that they may be welded into a unit because I am in them and You are in Me" (verses 20-23a).

All believers are to be one in spirit and purpose. He would have them be unified and keep on believing in the divine origin and mission of their Lord. He desires them to be molded into the one family of God. The moment they receive Christ, the Holy Spirit baptizes them into one body. All believers are as surely joined to one another as Jesus is to the Father.

His final request is that the men, who are the Father's gift to the Son, may be with Him to behold His glory, *"Father, they are Your gift to Me; and My desire is that they be with Me where I am, so they can see My glory, which You have given Me because You loved Me before the world began"* (vs. 24).

This is essential to their call. They are the first fruits of His mission in the world and they belong with Him in the life to come. Here we catch a glimpse of the warmth and depth of the Savior's love for the redeemed. He cannot bear to be without them, even though He will have the fellowship of the Father and the adoration of the angelic hosts. He is ready to assume possession of all the believers of all ages who have been given to Him as a gift by the Father. He will, at Pentecost; and once He does, they are sealed eternally (Ephesians 1:13-14).

After this unspeakably sublime consecration of His church, we listen to this, *"O, Righteous Father, it is true the world does not know You, but I do; and these men know You sent Me. I have revealed You to them and will continue to reveal You. I will do this so that Your love for Me may be in them, and I in them"* (verses 25-26).

Jesus has no thought of ever being separated from His own. The eternal safety of the disciples is sealed by this prayer. The climax in His Messianic appointment, the object of His rule over all mankind is the Father's gift of the unified church to Christ; and Christ gives eternal life to each person in that church. This is the charter of the church; her possession and joy; her faith, hope and love; and in this she is to stand, pray and work.

When our Lord and Savior finished His prayer, the apostles realized that it was not only for them, but for all of those who have loved Him from then until now, and for all who ever will love Him. One must read upon one's knees as we listen to our Lord praying for us, lifting us all up into the presence of His Father and ours. It gives one a sense of utter safety, for His prayer for us goes on night and day—forever. It is like arms about us, and because we choose to be His children and cling to Him, it will never let us go!

United In Love

The Father's gift to Christ was the unified church; our love for the unified church is our gift to Christ. The world will know we are Christians by the love we have for Jesus and each other; and the tolerance and compassion we have toward all people and other churches of different denominations. We feel a kinship which goes deeper and means more and lasts longer than all other relationships of life. Even death cannot break this tie which binds human hearts in Christian love. Believers can be separated by great distances from one another and may belong to different branches of the church, but these factors should not divide our essential unity in the Sprit that enables us to love one another.

As one in the Lord, we can all recapture the excitement of the early Christians and share the good news with the world. Pray that we may be one in spirit and purpose. Love is the greatest gift of all!

Spirit Power Action

You have just come from the innermost sanctuary of Christ. As He prayed for the unity of believers, may that be your prayer also. There is only one Spirit, one God, and one church: Protestant or Catholic, Pentecostal or conservative. God is bigger than any denominational differences. Christians are to look past petty doctrinal diversity that doesn't have to do with salvation and see what's in the heart. Whether or not a person loves the Lord and trusts Him for salvation are the only important issues; and only God knows when a person is truly saved. We are consecrated to continue the apostles' ministry of sharing the Gospel and revealing the glorious indwelling of Christ to the world.

For an in-depth study of the Master's life, words, and ministry as they occurred, get a **Harmony of the Gospels**, a book or Bible that combines and harmonizes the four Gospels, with parallel texts printed side by side and the Life of Christ in chronological order. Some study Bibles have a good harmony and commentary (**Life Application Bible** is excellent). You can use any translation you like. Two other useful reference books are a concordance and Bible dictionary. Pay particular attention to Jesus' words in the Sermon on the Mount and Heart of Christ. When His life is studied in chronological order and context, the Savior's words come alive in your heart and His ministry makes a lot more sense.

If you feel you have enough knowledge and the Spirit leads, teach a class on the Life of Christ, either in a small home gathering or church group. Interpret His life in your own style, possibly using audio and visual techniques, and other interesting props. By teaching, you'll learn even more about the wonderful Savior we have, and you'll find His words just as relevant and powerful today as they were 2,000 years ago. Jesus is the same yesterday, today and forever!

"Be brought into a real and actual union with Him and be at one with Him—one will, one purpose, one interest, one life. Human words cannot express such a glory as this. And yet it ought to be expressed, and our souls ought to be made so unutterably hungry to realize it, that day or night we shall not be able to rest without it." —Hannah Whitall Smith, from the book *The Christian's Secret of a Happy Life*

TEMPTATION OF JESUS IN THE WILDERNESS

Nine

BLESSED ARE THE OVERCOMERS

"The first man Adam became a living being. The last Adam became a life-giving spirit. The first man was of the earth, made of dust; the second man is the Lord from heaven" (1 Corinthians 15:45,47).

Christ, the Last Adam

About 4,000 years after what Adam had lost when He chose to disobey God and the resulting

101

consequences of sin, the promised Redeemer came. At about age 30, Jesus was baptized by John the Baptist. Immediately afterward, the voice of the Father and the Holy Spirit in the form of a dove anointed Him for His messianic work. This was the first time the Trinity came together on earth.

In Jesus' case, baptism was not an act of repentance, or acknowledgment of sin and washing away of all uncleanness as it had been with the others. His physical act of baptism represented the total cleansing of the spiritual baptism to come. Christ was the true Baptizer who would make it all possible. He would redeem humankind through His death and resurrection, and "baptize" by the Holy Spirit on the Day of Pentecost, bringing eternal life.

At His baptism, Jesus fulfilled all righteousness in His act of obedience under Jewish law. Then He was led by the Spirit into the wilderness to have His righteousness tested by the devil. It was an actual human experience, with the same test of obedience that Adam and Eve had failed in the Garden of Eden at the beginning.

Christ's Victories over the Devil

Jesus' temptation in the wilderness at the beginning of His ministry and His victory over the devil in the Garden of Gethsemane just before His arrest and crucifiction show us how to successfully resist the enemy without fear.

First Temptation in the Wilderness

At Christ's first temptation in the wilderness of Judea, He ate nothing for forty days and nights, and afterwards became very hungry. Then, at the Lord's weakest point, Satan tempted Him three times. In the first, the devil said, *"If You are the Son of God, tell these stones to become bread"* (Matthew 4:3).

The evil voice had dared to speak to Him in the words of Scriptures He loved. Jesus answered with Scripture, *"Man shall not live by bread alone, but by every word of God"* (vs. 4).

In the second temptation, the devil took Him to the Holy City on a pinnacle of the Temple and said, *"If You are the Son of God, throw Yourself down, for Scripture says, 'He will put His angels in charge of You, and they will support You'"* (vs. 6).

Jesus replied, *"You shall not put the Lord Your God to the test"* (vs. 7).

The third time Satan offered the whole world to the Person who had come to save it and offered to give it to Him—but there was a catch. Jesus had to obtain it by worshipping the devil and disobeying God.

Then the Son spoke directly to Satan with all the authority of His Father in heaven, backed by His

Holy Word, *"Go away, Satan!"* Jesus ordered. *"The Scripture says, 'You must worship the Lord your God; and serve only Him'"* (vs. 10). Jesus resisted, and immediately the evil one left Him. All three temptations had been overcome. Then angels attended to Christ's needs. The enemy departed from Him for only a season, and there would be echoes of temptation all of His life.

Last Temptation in Garden of Gethsemane

About three and one half years later, the devil was back at the next weakest point in Christ's life— moments before He was arrested and crucified. In the garden of Gethsemane, Jesus cried out three times to the Father to keep Him from the agony of the cross. He knew He would be separated from the Father for a period of time on it to pay for our sins, and that's what made this temptation the hardest of all.

In full view was the deepest mystery of our faith: the two natures in one person. His human nature could sin; His righteous nature could not. There would be no reason at all to tempt Jesus if He could not sin. Both natures spoke: one with, *"if it be possible to take this cup of suffering away from Me;"* and the other with His extreme obedience, *"not My will, but Yours be done"* (Luke 22:42).

Every time the Son said in obedience, *"Not My will, but Yours be done,"* Christ came forth triumphant! He had His last chance to walk away from it—but He didn't. The real war for our souls was fought and won here! In this other Eden, the second Adam, the Lord from heaven, bore the penalty of the first; and in obeying, redeemed mankind! The devil was vanquished and his fate was sealed shortly afterwards by Christ's victorious redemption and resurrection.

Could Jesus Sin?

All people are born with just one sinful nature. But Jesus was born with two natures, one that was righteous and could not sin, and the other with the ability to sin. Unlike us, His Father was God who gave Him a totally righteous nature unable to sin. However, like us, He also had a nature that was able to sin; inherited from the line of Adam through Mary His mother. He had the ability to sin, the same as we do, but He chose never to sin and always obey His Father. That is why He is the only righteous person in the world, and why only He could be the Redeemer and our High Priest (Hebrews 2:17; 4:14-15).

Christ's temptations were real and His resistance was real, and not merely acts of going through the motions. If He could not sin, we could never be like Him and the test would be worthless to us. His ability to sin is the reason Scripture says He was tempted in regard to all things in like manner as we, but without sin—and we can follow in His footsteps. Whatever Jesus overcame, we can overcome! His victory is ours with the power of His Holy Spirit!

Satan's Loss, Our Gain

At Calvary, Satan became a defeated enemy. Jesus' redemptive work on the cross sealed the devil's fate. The devil lost his claim to the souls of all "born from above" believers. We still have our old natures where Satan can tempt us, but are no longer slaves to them or the devil. Christ has set us free!

"He has delivered us from the power of darkness and conveyed us into the kingdom of the Son of His love, in whom we have redemption through His blood, the forgiveness of sins" (Colossians 1:13-14).

Our Victorious New Nature

When we were born to our earthly parents, we entered the world equipped with the nature they gave us, which was inherited from Adam and Eve. The old nature is born of the flesh and sins continually. It is where the devil accesses our minds and thoughts. All people start off with a sinful nature that ends in a double death—both physical and spiritual.

When we take Jesus as our Savior, we are born from above; we are a "new creation." This second birth gives us a new nature, the Lord's own nature, sealed by the Holy Spirit. Our new nature is righteous. It is where the Holy Spirit resides and where we have fellowship with God and have the power to defeat the devil. Since it is God's holy nature, the new nature cannot sin and this is the only nature we take with us to heaven. The only "death" we suffer is that of the body. We have everlasting life in the Spirit.

The mind of the Christian is free to choose between His two natures. These two natures explain why a Christian can sin at one moment and be righteous the next.

Satan Is Powerful, But Defeatable

Satan is the most powerful evil being in the universe. Only God (Holy Trinity) has the greater power to defeat him. Therefore, we can only be victorious over him through the greater power of the Holy Spirit within us. When we talk directly to Satan and conquer him, we automatically have dominion over all of his underlings: demons, fallen angels and beings, ghosts, spirits, and all of his other slaves in the spirit world.

Even though the devil is a defeated enemy through the Cross and no longer owns Christians' souls, he can tempt us to sin through our old natures. Obedience is not automatic; we can still disobey God. Life is a constant battle between good and evil. Resisting and overcoming are what make us righteous and rich in Spirit. You cannot ignore him and hope he will go away. You have to attack and defeat him every time. Not only that, you have to make sure he doesn't return or sneak back in with another evil idea.

Still Up to His Old Tricks

Watch out for the devil's disguises, deceptions and tricks that are even more subtle than the ones he used on Adam and Eve. Eating the fruit and the supposed "benefits" it would bring appeared to be good, but the First Pair should have rejected it because it was contrary to God's specific instructions. Evil thoughts can pop up into our minds from anywhere; so can evil suggestions from friends; even something that "appears" to be good may be from an evil source.

Anything that is contrary from what the Word of God says is the work of the devil. This is why Jesus used Scripture against him, and we should too. Instead of listening to the "father of lies," our Lord made him listen to "Scripture says…" The Bible is called the "sword of the Spirit" and we are authorized to use it on our enemy, the devil, who is determined to destroy us. The Lord's genius is that He uses someone as evil as Satan to make us victorious.

Always look at the source of any suspicious idea. Is it unknown or trustworthy? Is it of the Spirit or the devil? Does it honor God or yourself?

Spirit Power Action

Take authority over Satan! *"Resist the devil, and he will flee from you"* (James 4:7). Christians acting in the power of the Holy Spirit can take authority over him in the same way our Savior did. As a defeated enemy, Satan must obey us when we command him in Jesus' name to leave us alone.

Caution: Do not try this unless you are a Christian. The devil will laugh at anyone who does not have the power of God's Holy Spirit. Not sure? Go back to the end of Chapter 3 and confirm your salvation.

Step 1. Take control of what goes into your mind. BLOCK and eliminate all evil and negative assaults from entering your mind and life. These can be negative thoughts, emotions, sights, sounds, images, people's words. Ask the Spirit to help you instantly recognize any evil and negativity when it hits you. If something comes from Satan, catch him in the act. If you can detect him even as he deposits a suggestion in your mind, you've got him. Then you can defeat him. It's not hard to do if you are watching.

Move fast. You've caught him in the trap. You recognize his evil idea for what it does to your intention to obey the Lord. You've got him. Now defeat him by speaking directly to him, "Satan, I am acting with the authority of Jesus. Go away from me and take your deadly assaults with you. You will not destroy me with evil or negativity. I don't want any part of your lies; for Scripture says…(quote your favorite verses)!"

Every time he tempts you, tell him, **"no"** or **"stop"** to prevent him from doing a specific thing to your mind or body. Do this as many times as it takes. Constantly guard against any of the devil's temptations so they won't return. If you are persistent, he will see you are serious about this and eventually give up.

Have your favorite matching verses ready for each area of temptation and thrust God's Word toward Satan when attacked. Sometimes only one thrust of the "Sword of the Spirit" will be necessary to send him on his way. The devil is the only one on whom we are authorized to use God's Word as a weapon. He is the only enemy we need to defeat.

Don't be afraid; he can't hurt you. His power against you is limited to suggestion only. But that's hard enough. Remember, you have the greater authority and power through the Holy Spirit. The devil is a defeated enemy and he has to leave. All the power of heaven is backing you. God has promised strength in your weakness.

Step 2. Nature hates a vacuum, and so does God. When you cast off evil and negativity, a vacuum of sorts is created. The devil would love to regain that ground. But no military leader is eager to spill additional blood to take the same hill a second time. As General Patton said, "I don't like to pay for the same real estate twice." And when that vacuum is filled with Jesus, Satan cannot retake the ground.

"And do not be conformed to this world, but be transformed by the renewing of your mind, that you may prove what is that good and acceptable and perfect will of God" (Romans 12:2).

Now FILL your mind with only righteous, positive thoughts, sights, sounds, images, electronic media, books—especially the Bible, and encouraging words from friends and family. Surround yourself with positive people who inspire you. These are your true friends. Pray in the soul sanctuary of your imagination and ask God to help you completely heal your mind and body. Let your spirit soar as you stay close to Jesus and are mindful of His indwelling presence. Soon you will see a dramatic attitude shift to positive, and your mind and body will start to heal. You will thrill to the Spirit's power and God's Word as they do their work before your eyes.

A renewed mind, wealth of spirit, wellness of body, strengthening of faith, and outpouring of creativity are just a few of the blessings. Your mind and body are functioning at full capacity, finding solutions to problems, and producing a vast quantity of creative new ideas. You may discover you have more than one creative or spiritual gift.

Conquerors in Christ

"He who overcomes, I will grant to him to sit down with Me on My throne, as I also overcame and sat down with My Father on His throne" (Revelation 3:21).

Success reaps great rewards for overcomers— both in this life and the next. Once you taste victory and power over Satan, your life is never the same. All weaknesses and evil situations are turned into the glory of God. You have exercised your power to change into the likeness of Christ and He becomes more real to you. With each conquest comes the reward of a changed life. You are able to fulfill your destiny and calling to the fullest measure!

"For I am persuaded that neither death, nor life, nor angels, nor principalities, nor powers, nor things present, nor things to come, nor height, nor depth, nor any other created thing, shall be able to separate us from the love of God which is in Christ Jesus our Lord" (Romans 8:38-39.

WORD OF LIFE--SERMON ON THE MOUNT

Ten

DON'T WORRY—BE HAPPY!

"You will keep in perfect peace all who trust in You, whose thoughts are fixed on You" (Isaiah 26:3).

Don't Worry

It is possible to be free of worry and live a happy life! Jesus devoted His ministry to assure us that it was true. His words on the Sermon on the Mount are the most beautiful plan for the worry-free life. Spiritual concerns are to override physical concerns about life and possessions.

Take a step back in time about 2,000 years ago. It is a warm sunny day in Israel and Jesus is standing on a hill above the Sea of Galilee facing a large crowd of people gathered below. A spring breeze from the lake brushes the faces of the multitude looking up at the Lord. They have come to hear what He has to say, totally unaware of the power of the words about to fall on their ears. "Shhhh," the people say to each other, and a hush settles over them.

The Master speaks:

"Listen carefully: do not worry about staying alive that you become anxious over food and drink. God has given you life and a body, and they are far more important than what to eat or what to wear. If He can give you life, He can certainly provide what is needed for your existence. Look at the wild birds. They do not worry about sowing or reaping or storing food. They do not have to; your Heavenly Father feeds them. And you are worth far more to Him than they are. So how can worrying about these things add anything to your life?

"Are not two sparrows sold for a penny? Yet not even one of them falls to the earth without your Father's knowledge. As for you, even the hairs of your head have all been counted. Therefore, stop being afraid! You are worth more than any number of sparrows.

"And why worry about your clothes? Look at the wild lilies of the field and how they grow. They do not work or make their clothing, yet Solomon in all his splendor was

never dressed as beautifully as one of these. Therefore, if God clothes the flora of the field with such dazzling beauty, which is here today and gone tomorrow; He will most certainly clothe you. You have so little faith!

"Do not worry about having enough food or drink or clothing. That is what the heathen do. Your heavenly Father already knows all your needs, and He will give you all you need from day to day if you live for Him and make the Kingdom of God your primary concern. Store up treasures in heaven where their value remains forever and there is no way to lose them. For where your treasure is, there will your heart be also.

"So do not worry about tomorrow. Just live one day at a time and deal with one day's troubles. God will take care of tomorrow as surely as He is taking care of today" (Matthew 6:25-34).

When Christ's last words echoed across the fields, the people didn't move. They were frozen to the spot, astonished and dumbfounded. Then they asked one another, "What was it about this man that warmed our hearts so? What made His words so compelling, so believable?" It seemed as if God had spoken directly to them—and they were right! He had just revealed the secrets of the Kingdom of Heaven. It was personal, inward and spiritual.

The same Jesus who ministered to the crowd that day still speaks to us. And when He does, God's Word has the same stunning effect on all who hear it. We're not like those at the foot of the hill in Galilee wondering why His words were so compelling. We know why—Jesus is God, and His words are the words of God that change our lives forever!

Peace of God

On the eve of His crucifixion, Christ reassured His disciples, *"My peace I give to you, such as the world cannot give. Set your troubled hearts at rest, and banish your fears"* (John 14:27).

The peace of God is one of the major themes of the Bible. It is designed to fit precisely into our basic spiritual needs. It is beyond all understanding, which means no one will ever be able to comprehend this great gift. Reason may not be able to grasp it, but faith can; and we don't have to understand it to enjoy its benefits. It isn't something to rationalize, but to simply believe.

A heartwarming story of peace is depicted in a painting of a severe storm. The blowing wind and the driving rain made it almost impossible to see the small chicken coop near a farmhouse. Suddenly a lightning bolt struck near the wood shelter and illuminated the inside where a hen was setting on her nest. Though the storm was all around, the mother hen's chicks were sheltered under her wings, totally protected from the storm and at peace with the world. The painting was called "Perfect Peace."

We can live in the world and not be the victim of it because we belong to God. He longs to gather us beneath His wings to make everything right, no matter how wrong it may appear. God is our shelter in the storm, refuge and strength, and help in time of trouble. He will keep us in perfect peace if we keep our minds on Him (Psalm 46:1; Isaiah 26:3).

Paul tells us, *"The Lord is near; do not be anxious, but in everything make your requests known to God in prayer and petition with thanksgiving. Then the peace of God, which is beyond all understanding, will guard your hearts and minds through Christ Jesus"* (Philippians 4:6-7).

Things that happen to believers are not accidents; they are either allowed or sent by our Father in heaven. There is nothing that strengthens Christians' hearts and faith and brings peace in times of adversity than knowing God participates in every detail of our lives. Those of us who are privileged to know something of Christ's working find great comfort in knowing that "this thing is from God" and that the Sovereign Lord will work this thing together for our good and for His glory. His faithfulness continues without interruption, even if we fall back into the old rut of rebellion and worry. It is extremely comforting to know that we will never experience a problem, trial, or heartache beyond the control of God.

Many pressures are upon us as we rush around trying to live and raise our families in today's world. When things get tough and trouble closes in, believers are often stressed and full of anxiety over finances, relationships, work, and many other problems. We can lose sight of our Lord's closeness and guidance, and take the burdens on our own shoulders. Because worry is such a destructive force on our minds and bodies, we can actually be worried to death. However, most of our problems are really minor, and we tend to worry over nothing. Most of the things we worry about never actually happen. When they do, they are never as bad as our fear of them. We don't have to be in such a sorry state, because there is a simple solution.

Cast Your Cares on Jesus

"Give over to Him all of your cares and anxieties, for He cares for you and is in complete control of every circumstance of your life" (1 Peter 5:7).

Jesus is in control, and we are to cast our cares upon His broad shoulders when the burden becomes too much to bear. Accept His invitation, *"Come unto me, all that labor and are heavy laden, and I will give you rest"* (Matthew 11:28). After taking on the burden of the world's sins at His crucifixion, our miniscule problems are nothing to Him. The secret is to turn our problems over to the Lord before they become overbearing—instead of using Him as the only option left. After we've done all we can do, all we have to say is, "Jesus, this problem is beyond me and there's nothing more I can do. I trust you to take care of it." He is right there to help us find the remedy and guide us through any trial and adversity.

The joy of living free from worry and fear is possible only if we cast our burdens upon God, and continue to do so daily. He will either prevent all adversity or turn it to our profit. For if God governs our lives, or if we commit ourselves to Him, we are in the hands of the One who has complete mastery of all things and therefore conquers all worries.

Be Happy

The Lord's ultimate goal is to teach us to be joyful and praise Him in spite of the circumstances. Everyone can praise Him when things are going good. But how many can when things are bad? Only in the power of the Holy Spirit can we do this. Believers are to praise Him and have joy—no matter what. We are to come to Him with all the details of our lives—both hard and happy times.

Christians who have immeasurable difficulties can have smiles on their faces with no complaining, moaning or groaning, and at the same time thank God, knowing He will see them through. Those who have learned to focus on the Savior know He is in the process of conforming them to His image in the midst of trouble. His faithfulness becomes their strength and they do not suffer defeat.

We all have worries every day, but Jesus promises to remain with us when troubles come. Our problems should never weigh us down, especially as we realize He is sharing the burden with us. We have an omnipotent God who walks with us. With the Lord's help you can overcome worry, phobias, evil thoughts, destructive emotions, circumstances, and lifestyle—anything that enslaves and prevents you from fulfilling the work God has given you to do. And you will be extremely happy!

Live Above Your Circumstances

"Life isn't about waiting for the storm to pass, but learning how to dance in the rain." —Vivian Greene

Here are simple steps for joyful living above all circumstances:

1. Rejoice over what is being accomplished, sing praises even if you don't feel like it. Thank God instead of complaining. When He's finished using the circumstances, He'll alter them.

2. Don't focus on the causes or how they affect you. "Pity Parties" don't solve anything and only show lack of faith.

3. In seeking happiness for others, we find it ourselves. Help someone in a worse situation than you. Share the life-changing message of Christ. Make the Gospel and the Kingdom of God your primary concern.

4. Look for opportunities to demonstrate the power of the Holy Spirit to carry you through your circumstances. How you react to adversity is noticed by everyone around you.

5. Submit yourself to the will of the Father. Believe God will bring you through circumstances. Jesus is the buffer, except when He allows them, and He will do whatever it takes for you to be conformed to the image of His Son. Resist any of the devil's negative thoughts and suggestions, and when you do, he will stop and leave you alone.

6. All of us have favorite Bible verses God brings to mind whenever we face difficulties. Make a list of promise verses and praise songs for every situation and have it handy. With each victory it will become more automatic and your joy will be overflowing!

Spirit Power Action

Create a soul sanctuary, a peaceful room or space in your home, or an outside garden grotto that is a shelter from the storms of life. You can decorate the area with inspiring art and objects, and play peaceful music. It is a private holy place where you daily recharge your soul, read Scripture, find your promise verses and praise songs, and talk to the Lord. Start by committing at least five minutes a day to Him. Once you see how comforting and inspiring Scripture is and how God's words come alive with the Spirit revealing their meaning, you'll discover how much you enjoy the Lord. You will want to spend even more time alone with Him each day. Then you'll be ready to face the world and whatever difficulty it might bring.

Here's how to find the perfect study Bible just for you:

First, go to a local bookstore with a good variety of Bibles. Select several excellent modern-day translations you easily understand, and sample the same portion in each translation. You will immediately see the difference in each. Jesus' words are best for this test. Buy the translation that speaks to your heart the most, or buy several to compare as you study. Each study Bible has different features, so don't limit yourself to just one translation and study guide. The **Life Application Bible** is an outstanding study Bible that comes in several translations.

Second, select a chapter to read. There is no set rule stating you have to start with the book of Genesis. Since the Bible is a collection of books, you can start almost anywhere. I recommend you first choose the four Gospels in the New Testament; a good order is John, Matthew, Mark, Luke, and Acts (which is a continuation of Luke). Follow this by Romans and the rest of Paul's letters.

After completing the New Testament, it is a good time to start Genesis and read stories of people of faith, such as Adam and Eve, Noah, Abraham, Joseph,

Moses, Ruth, David, and Daniel. Then enjoy the wonderful Psalms which give you comfort in times of trouble, and a sense of what it means to praise and worship God. Some of the world's best poetry is there. As you read, you will see how Old Testament events and prophecies lead up to Christ.

Third, before each reading, ask the Holy Spirit to reveal the hidden secrets of God, the person of Jesus, and what the Kingdom of God is really like, and He will—it's His ministry! Then you will be able to see with the "eyes of your heart" and marvel at the wisdom the Word brings to your life.

"Calmness in the midst of turmoil, absence of worry or anxiety, deliverance from care and fear—all these and many other similar graces, are invariably found to be the natural outward development of that inward life which is hid with Christ in God." –Hannah Whitall Smith, from the book *"The Christian's Secret of a Happy Life"*

LIGHT OF LIFE

Eleven

LET YOUR LIGHT SHINE

"Let your light shine before men, that they may see your good deeds and praise your Father in heaven" (Matthew 5:16).

Friends Are Gifts from God

Who would suspect that the ability to make friends is an enviable gift of God? The ability to show tender sympathy toward a burdened heart is surely a choice gift. What about those traits which make people feel wanted and important? They can be used to reveal Christ's boundless gifts. Who has not reveled in the charm of, "I know how you feel?" Simple words, but they communicate fireside warmth to an aching soul. More than one child has quieted his fluttering heart by mother's tender, "There, there, mother understands." Should not others also experience this

125

revelation through personal contact? Sharing God's love and compassion is always best served through person-to-person contact.

The list of personal gifts is long. Your ministry may use many of them. There is no limit to the number of people you can serve—Christians or not! When you discover the power you receive from the Spirit as you go forth helping people, and the blessings you receive in return, you will want to serve Christ even more.

Naturally, Satan would work to conceal this blessedness. He fears an awakened and excited Christian multitude could destroy his plans more than anything else. Therefore, he diligently labors to conceal one of the most surprising features of all— the fact that you can serve our Lord and Savior at whatever level of ability that makes you comfortable. Not everyone can be Billy Graham, and you don't have to be. Just doing your very best with the ability you have been given is all God requires.

How to Make People Feel Comfortable in Your Presence

Making people feel comfortable in your presence is another gift from God. You can develop a personality that makes people feel perfectly at ease in your presence and non-threatened in any way. If you can get a person to relax and behave in his most natural manner when he is with you, your presence will be a great comfort and blessing to him, and your life will be flooded with new friends.

Here are six tips that allow others to be comfortable in your presence:

1. Kind eyes. Start off with a genuine smile as you look someone in the eyes with a non-threatening manner. As the most unpromising piece of ground may be the hiding place of the finest gold, so might the most humble person become the wealth of a new friend. The "Hello," that greets you in return could easily bring a precious colleague into your life. Meet with expectancy the face that appears, for behind it could be the sweetest treasure of a soul. God delights in giving us new friends. Train your eyes to discover things in people that are worthy of praise. Usually, we are so interested in ourselves that we miss most of what is so worthwhile in others.

2. Hearing ears. Dedicated ears are needed to listen to people's cry for help. Preaching gifts are exciting, but who will become God's ear? Many want to speak for Him, but who will listen for Him? The surrender of one's ears offers a listening gift that can bring the sweetest kind of healing. The apostle James knew this, *"Confess your sins one to another and pray for one another that you may be healed"* (James 5:16). In this busy world, God needs listeners as badly as preachers. You cannot begin to estimate the healing that comes from this type of service. Regard your ears to be as important as your lips. People love to talk about themselves, so be a good listener.

3. Encouraging Words. No one is ever happier than when he meets someone who displays genuine interest in him as a person. People long to be accepted by others, and a word of honest praise can satisfy that hunger quicker than anything else. Suppress the desire to speak of yourself and your own ideas unless they are asked for. Even then, make it brief and not too impressive. Build up your friend instead of yourself; you already know who you are in Christ. The more important a Christian really is, the more willing he should be to show interest in someone else. Your own importance will be communicated by your confident compassionate manor.

4. Don't react negatively. Find a way to agree with a person in general, even if you cannot agree with him in particular. If you correct someone, you will at once make him out to be wrong. For now, the relationship between you and your friend is more important than accuracy. Permit your friend his incorrectness and indicate your acceptance of him as an individual without revealing your feelings concerning error. "That's an interesting point of view," or "You certainly have a unique approach to the matter," are answers that appear to accept a person while not commenting directly on his opinion.

5. Hot topics burn friendships. Change the subject immediately if a hot topic is introduced into the conversation about which you have powerful feelings. Politics and religion are two biggies. Ask another question or change the subject. If he refuses to leave the matter, then handle yourself in a way that will not reveal your feelings. For example, if a person should say, "I think the Bible is 90% fiction," you could offer, "Well, at least that leaves us 10% to work with, should we decide to get into a discussion about it sometime." Though you may not agree with his thinking at all, you have still indicated an acceptance attitude. Touchiness is conceit set with a hair trigger.

6. Only give advice when asked for it. As your friendship increases and you know the person's attitude on certain subjects, you might be able to give informed advice. Only give advice when someone asks for it; then you can politely suggest, "I have some ideas that may help, if you are open to them." If the person says no, then stop.

Do the same when sharing the Gospel. If the person says, "I'd like to hear your ideas," or "Go ahead," relax and let the Spirit do the work naturally. All you have to do is be ready to share whatever the person is willing to receive. When the Holy Spirit asks you to speak or act, He anoints your words and deeds to that person's heart. You must be dedicated to the Lord Jesus and not use your power for selfish advantage. Otherwise, the Holy Spirit cannot bless your life. You can be the complete master of the situation, but you must reflect the gentle graciousness of the miracle of the indwelling Christ.

Pursuit of Excellence

Anyone can let their light shine, both inside and outside the church. The call of God always is in line with what a person can do and what he likes to do. This is good economy on the part of the Lord, for no one stays long on a job that he dislikes and which is beyond his ability.

Right now dear reader, estimate your abilities and see what type of ministry best suits you. This can be in addition to your primary calling. Don't underestimate your talents. Many people have several gifts. Why not give the matter some thought? You have nothing to lose and there is no reason why you shouldn't be enjoying at least one, or more, Christ-honoring ministries. It would be most proper for you to consider anyplace where the Spirit leads you to work. Answering these questions will help you get started:

1. What am I doing for Christ today?

2. Do I have a real ministry that employs the talents He has given me and where I can use them to the fullest?

3. Would I be willing to use my gifts in both Christian and non-Christian endeavors?

4. If a little time spent in training would insure my success, would I be willing to spend it?

Here are **three levels of ministry** that let your light shine on the good news of Jesus Christ:

Level 1. Make It a Specialty to Help Someone in Need

"Let each of us please his neighbor for his good, to build him up" (Romans 15:2).

Simply help people for the sheer joy of it. You don't even have to say a word about Jesus; your Christ-like actions speak louder than words. Here are some needs you can fill:

A.   Visit the sick, comfort the lonely and elderly.

B.   Take a person under your wing for mentoring.

C.   Open your home for counseling and study groups.

D.   Use your motor vehicle to shuttle nondrivers and other people in your area who lack transportation.

E.   Make a comforting call or send a cheerful email to distressed persons.

F.   Assist a family who needs help with food, shelter, clothing, and bill-paying. Many social services are available and you can refer them to the right agency.

G.   Act as a peacemaker between quarrelsome family members or friends—if they ask you for help.

Level 2. Witnessing for Christ

"You shall be my witnesses...even in the farthest corners of the earth" (Acts 1:8).

The Lord is aware of variables in His people. He knows some are endowed with public gifts, while others are shy and timid. That's why He gave the command to witness. Everyone can witness, even though not all go on to win souls. Why? There are ways to witness that match the shyness of the most timid soul. Everyone can begin witnessing with the easiest steps; and then, with the passing of time, graduate to harder ones.

Here are three easy steps to help build your skills. Start slowly and work up to where you feel most comfortable. When you accomplish this, other ideas will come to mind. Remember, no preaching—just natural conversation friend to friend. Always be ready for an opportunity to share when a person asks a question or needs your help.

The first step is to **wear or display a symbol of faith** so that others can identify you as a person who believes in God. There are many pins and necklaces with Christian symbols that tell people you are a person of faith. They are fun to wear, and attractive. Some Christians have stickers and even website addresses on their vehicles. People in the vehicles next to you have time to read them at light signals. Don't overdo anything that would make you look like a religious fanatic. Your true inner joy will attract many to ask why you are so happy.

The second step is to **give a thoughtful gift**. A friend or person you work with may mention he (or she) needs an item or wishes he could have something in particular. The Lord may lay it on your heart to give a certain gift to someone. It may, or may not, be overtly Christian; it's the thoughtfulness behind it that counts. When presenting it, just say, "I thought you'd like to have this," or whatever words are appropriate. Don't say any more about it unless asked. Each time the person uses the gift, he is reminded of your kind act, and later may ask you more about your faith.

The third step is to **share what God has done for you.** It can be verbal, a personal letter, or email. Almost everyone asks, "How are you, how is everything going, or what's new with you?" Use traditional forms of communication, or internet technology that goes all over the world. If someone mentions a problem or illness in his family, reply by saying you will pray for that person. You can reach more people for Christ than you ever thought possible. Put a cheery voicemail message on your phone. This is witnessing and it is thrilling!

Witnessing on the job. In today's world of political and religious correctness, more and more companies do not want Christians talking about Christ to other employees. They have a right to make their own rules. A wise servant learns how to serve Christ within company rules. He keeps the rules as faithfully as any other employee. It is part of his stewardship to comply with company policy and he does so unto the Lord. The Lord is not honored by a disagreeable employee. If he is told not to speak of Christ, he complies. If he feels he can't, then he should quit the job.

But this isn't the end of the matter. There are many ways to identify with Jesus within company rules. Every time anyone asks, "Hi, how are you today?" He can reply: "I am fine, thank the Lord," and back it up with a huge smile. Unconsciously, the Lord is credited with the light shining from such a servant. The Holy Spirit sees to it. The tremendous spirit of a true Christian cannot be concealed. He overflows with joy; he glows with the adventure of serving Jesus. Company rules don't slow him down at all. They simply challenge his resourcefulness in the Spirit. Then, when people have problems, whom do you think they come to see? That's right, the Christian! He can't be blamed when people come asking him for help or inquiring about his joy.

If it costs him his job to be identified with Christ, so be it. God will have an even better job waiting for him. Throughout the ages, true servants have paid a price for their identification with Christ, and have been counted worthy to bear the reproach of the Lord and share in His sufferings. Like Apostle Paul, they count it an honor.

Level 3. Soul-Winning

"For out of the abundance of the heart the mouth speaks. The good person out of his good treasure brings forth good" (Matthew 12:34-35).

Some people have gifts of presenting Christ to another person directly, and they make it their specialty. A faithful stewardship of talents like these will not allow them to be satisfied with serving Jesus at a different level. A person's gifts are appointed by the Lord, not of his own choosing. Therefore, the work to which one is called cannot be rated above that of another. This truth should be clearly in view.

It is the ultimate thrill to watch a soul enter God's family. To look upon one that you have personally introduced to Jesus, sends the heart on a heavenly flight. The apostle Paul referred to his converts as his "joy and crown." What a reward to spend eternity with those you have led to Jesus!

Learn how to introduce a person to Christ, even if you can't do it right now. It's as easy as telling someone that Jesus died for him so that he might have the free gift of eternal life. His sins will be forgiven by inviting Jesus into his heart with a simple prayer. The Spirit is the real worker. You only have to be ready. The message is simply John 3:16 in a nutshell, and helping a person to be born from above is really the ultimate thrill of all Christianity.

As you help those who need Jesus, you might come in contact with a dying person crying out to be saved, or someone might come to you and ask how to become a Christian. The Spirit will urge you when to offer Christ's invitation. This is soul-winning and the ultimate joy! Just ask the individual if he would like to receive God's free gift of eternal life. No fancy words or ceremonies are needed; just plain talk with another about the Lord.

If the person's answer is yes, ask him to repeat the "sinner's prayer" along with you in small steps, "Dear Jesus, I confess that I am a sinner and ask for your forgiveness. By faith, I invite you into my heart as my Savior and Lord. I receive your free gift of eternal life."

The actual words don't matter to God, only what's in the heart. Just make sure the person understands a new birth is happening inside him. If you have further contact, you can help the new Christian grow in the Lord. If the individual says no, that's OK too. Don't press, he may change his mind later.

When you get to heaven, there will be many new believers who come to you and say, "I want to thank you for sharing your faith. You are the one responsible for my being here." What a celebration that will be!

Andrew Murray offered this of his own life, "The higher I rise in the consciousness of being like Christ, the deeper shall I stoop to serve all around me." How like the Savior! *For even the Son of Man did not come to be served, but to give His life as a ransom for many*" (Mark 10:45). Self-denial is the principle motif of the Christian's character. The crown of a useful life is not to acquire as much influence as possible, but to throw it away and let it disappear into the lives of others.

Spirit Power Action

"To me, who am less than the least of all the saints, this grace was given, that I should preach among the Gentiles the unsearchable riches of Christ" (Ephesians 3:8).

How you present yourself to the world is extremely important to your testimony. As a representative of the Kingdom of God, your own appearance needs to reflect the unfathomable riches in Christ. Have the personal appearance of a child of the King, no matter your income level; money is not the issue for the rich in Spirit. You are a reflection of God, and your home and material possessions are a reflection of you. All these things need to be kept clean and bright to shine for God's glory. When people drive by your exceptionally maintained home and surroundings, they will remark, "That's the home of a Christian." When you invite people inside, the peace and serenity of God will astound them.

Be an outstanding citizen, personally involved in community good works. Be a good neighbor, willing to help at a moment's notice. Honesty, integrity and reliability are your middle names. This reinforces your testimony.

Here are the steps:

1. Make people feel comfortable in your presence, then go help them.
2. Match your gifts with your level of Christian ministry, then go do it.
3. Be a worthy representative of God's Kingdom. Let the Light of Life shine through you, then all the world can see Him.

God's children are like a lighthouse on a hill shining over a world of people plunged in darkness. Radiate Christ's good news of eternal life, then some of them may come to you and ask how to have it for themselves!

"…you shine like stars in the universe as you hold out the Word of Life" (Philippians 2:15-16).

ON TOP OF THE WORLD

Twelve

PEOPLE OF POWER

"But one thing I do: Forgetting what is behind and straining toward what is ahead, I press towards the finish line to win the heavenly prize to which God has called me in Christ Jesus" (Philippians 3:13-14).

As runners approach the finish line, they don't slow down. When they see that tape, they run even harder. They have "one track minds." The same is true for Christians. A committed believer allows nothing to interfere with his dash to the finish line and win his heavenly prize. The steps in this book provide excellent training and preparation for the spiritual riches to come and an honored place at Jesus' side.

Peter and Paul's Power

Acts of the Apostles leaves no doubt that Peter, Paul, and the other disciples interpreted the whole Gospel to include miracles as manifestation of Christ's power working through them. His Holy Spirit endows His beloved children with the kind of faith and determination it takes to move mountains. Jesus made it perfectly clear: the greater the faith we have, the greater the gifts, power and miracles.

As long as the Holy Spirit indwells Christians on earth and until Christ returns in glory, all the spiritual gifts bestowed on believers at Pentecost are still in use. The reason we don't see them very often today is due to lack of faith in individual Christians; not because they have been withdrawn. All the power of God is still available to those who believe. Small miracles occur every day in our lives if we just look for them. Many are going on behind the scenes such as keeping us from accidents, coincidental meetings or events, unexplained circumstances which open doors or provide for daily needs.

Call to Action

We must take advantage of this remarkable time of human history in the age of the Holy Spirit. Such a thing has never happened before this age, nor will it happen afterwards. This is a truly unique period in the plan of God, and you and I are privileged to be a part of it.

Peter and Paul set the standard of what miracles, and also what hardships, we can expect when moving in the Spirit's power—and what great legacies we can leave to those who follow us.

Today, new chapters of Acts are being written as people of all ages receive Christ and His presence radiates through their lives. He continues to raise up all those of faith who are ready to do His will, and is just as eager to impart His power to us as He was through His apostles, and all those early Christians who shared their faith throughout the world.

I believe God is empowering a whole new generation for this end time. New talented leaders (young Peters and Pauls), filled with the Holy Spirit and faith, will emerge from them to lead the church, ignite the fire of Pentecost and once again show forth the Light of Life to this darkened world. You may be one of those whom God has called who will carry the banner for the next generation. We all have the opportunity to participate in it.

With the Spirit's anointing, believers can use all of their gifts. The possibilities are endless. Evangelists, writers, teachers, pastors with courage to speak out against evil will provide spiritual and moral leadership. An exciting life awaits those who listen to His voice, act on His words, and dare to be different. If we build our lives on those words, we will be different, no doubt about it. As children of God, we can speak those same words in Jesus' authority, and through the Holy Spirit's power, our ministries will come alive—and we will become more like Christ than we ever imagined!

Stand Up for What You Believe!

"Therefore, my beloved brethren, be steadfast, immovable, always abounding in the work of the Lord, knowing that your toil is not in vain in the Lord" (1 Corinthians 15:58).

There is plenty of work left to be done. Some say America is a post-constitutional country. Others say we are in a post-Christian society. I think both are true. The tide of evil is sweeping over the world and throwing it into darkness at a rapid pace. We know we are in the last days before Christ's glorious return to set things right. Watch for increasing persecution of Christians worldwide who will once again be martyred for their faith in the Lord.

Stand with someone who is being persecuted for the Gospel. Never fail to defend a brother or sister who is unjustly criticized or persecuted, rather than sentencing him to silence.

"Let us not become weary in doing good, for at the proper time we will reap a harvest if we do not give up" (Galatians 6:9).

The harvest is ripe! Use your talents and fulfill your calling while there is still time. Let your light shine on this darkened world so that it points the way to the Savior. God will give you the words to say and what to do when the situation needs it. Faith has no fear. The Lord is with you always. The truth will set the people free.

Let a Christian speak out for Jesus in the world, and he enters a wonderland where all things are changed by the power of God. It is a glorious kind of excitement that lasts. A believer may find astonishing wisdom on his lips, or see doors fling open that others said could never be opened. He will find himself doing things for the Lord he thought he could never do. He will see hardhearted and rugged people weep before his words, and find himself in the midst of miracle situations. A new glory fills his soul; he has entered into the highest calling!

Have the faith to put your gifts into action. Go and He will go with you! Your heavenly prize is waiting for you. Cross that finish line a winner! You've earned the crown of righteousness!

Spirit Power Action

Leave a legacy. You have found your true calling and are fulfilling your purpose in life. You are a person who knows who he is in Christ, has the power of the Holy Spirit backing him up, is leading a life pleasing to God, and knows that a wealth of spirit awaits him in eternity.

Your life's great work and knowledge must be preserved and passed on to help all those who come after you. Now your goal is to instruct those of the next generation to continue your work. Godly children are a gift from God. Your gift to them is a firm foundation in Christ. Fully train them in the ways of the Lord. They are your legacy.

The Holy Spirit is Christ's legacy. Paul's magnificent letters to the churches of his day about the work of the Holy Spirit are a wealth of information, and are his legacy. How little we would know about the Spirit without them.

Do you know what your legacy is? What is your great work that you want to pass on? Having a will (or family trust) on paper is good for making things legal, but also be sure to express your wishes to a trustworthy steward before you leave this world. These two things will insure that your legacy is carried out.

"All we have is today. Our challenge is to live it as if it were our last and to live it to the fullest." – Lloyd John Ogilvie

TRIUNE GOD (FATHER, SON, HOLY SPIRIT)

Thirteen

BELIEVERS' GREATEST EVENT

"Take heart! I have overcome the world" (John 16:33).

Over 2,000 years ago Jesus said, *"I have the power to lay down My life, and have the power to take it up again"* (John 10:18). On a late Friday afternoon He laid down His life, and early on the following

Sunday morning, He took it up again. Christ's resurrection at Easter proved He had the power, and in all of history, there has never been an event like it. Jesus crushed sin with His crucifixion, and death with His resurrection. We have eternal life because He has conquered death and has given us His Holy Spirit. The risen Christ is the good news of eternal life.

"I'll Be Back!"

On the day of His ascension, Jesus lead His disciples to Bethany, on the eastern slope of the Mount of Olives outside Jerusalem. From there they went to the place of His ascension where He would make a visible and triumphal entry into heaven. On top of the mount, as the Lord spoke, He lifted His hands in blessing upon them; and while they were watching, He was taken up into a cloud and disappeared.

As the disciples were straining their eyes to see Him, two white-robed men suddenly stood there among them. They said, *"Men of Galilee, why are you standing here staring at the sky? Jesus has been taken away from you into heaven. Someday, just as you saw Him go, He will return"* (Acts 1:11). The two angels spoke the prophecy that He would come back in like manner on this very spot as "King of Kings" and "Lord of Lords."

Triumphal Return

"When Christ, who is our Life shall appear, then we shall also appear with Him in glory. We shall be like Him, for we shall see Him as He is" (Colossians 3:4; 1 John 3:2).

Appearing with Jesus in glory at the First Resurrection (rapture) is the believers' greatest event! At the end of this age, Jesus' spectacular return will be like lightning flashing across the sky. The "King of Kings" and "Lord of Lords" makes a visible and triumphal entry back into time and space, descending into the clouds over the Mount of Olives. But He's not alone when He returns. In a flash, a "twinkling of an eye," the whole family of God is suddenly in the sky with Him.

Two things happen simultaneously at the return of Christ and resurrection of believers (First Resurrection): the **rapture**, catching away of what's left of the church on earth at that time; and the **resurrection** of God's family who had previously died. The instant Jesus appears in the sky, the saints still alive on earth are with Him. It won't matter what they're doing; they all are instantly caught up into the clouds. All believers who died before this event instantly leave heaven, and return to time and appear with Jesus in the sky (Matthew 24:30; 1 Thessalonians 4:15-17; Revelation 19:11-16; 20:6).

What a grand celebration! The whole church is united with the Lord in the sky. We're with all our loved ones in Christ who ascended to glory ahead of us. Heroes of the faith are there as well. All believers from Adam to the last person named in the Lamb's Book of Life are part of it, and appear in their new supernatural resurrection bodies. In the midst of all these people is the Lord Jesus appearing in the glory of His Father. Best of all, we're with Jesus face to face, hearing His voice, looking into His eyes, and seeing the love He has for us. We will never be separated from this moment on (Revelation 19:11-16; Matthew 16:27; 1 Thessalonians 3:13).

Before Jesus and all the saints descend to earth, several things happen. Christ's first task is to judge His beloved people for their works and distribute His rewards among them. The rewards are positions in Jesus' kingdom, which are assigned on the basis of each person's faithfulness to His calling. This is separate from salvation, which is a free gift from God. Judgment of Christians and assignment of positions in the kingdom are instantly accomplished.

But the terrified unsaved people who are watching from below realize it is no ordinary cloud; this is a cloud of Christians, so many in fact, they appear as a cloud. Jesus really is who He said He is. But it's too late for the people left behind to be saved. The Age of the Holy Spirit has ended, and along with it, salvation by faith. Christ's church is already complete. God knows beforehand who will be saved and who won't, and He is just in His judgment (1 Corinthians 15:20-28; 2 Corinthians 5:10; Revelation 7:9-17; Revelation 14:14-20).

No Christians ever receive the wrath of God! While all believers safely remain suspended in the clouds, Christ pours out His wrath and judges the unsaved people still remaining on earth. The unbelieving people are terrified of the "Righteous

Judge" who comes to pass judgment on them and remove all evil from the world. Jesus and His armies of heaven destroy Satan's armies at the Battle of Armageddon, wiping the scourge of evil from the face of the earth. Satan is bound and later sentenced and punished after the millennium.

Kingdom Come—the Millennium

After cleansing the earth, actually the whole physical universe, all creation is restored to its former glory as God created it in the beginning. The Garden of Eden has come full circle. An era of peace now begins.

Now the cloud of Christians descends around the Mount of Olives, King Jesus takes His rightful place in Jerusalem, and we take our places at His side in the Kingdom of God during Christ's millennial reign.

The millennial kingdom is Christ's inheritance from His Father, and we are "joint-heirs" with Him. He earned it, freed us, and presented His complete church to the Father. We are priests of God and of Christ and reign with Him a thousand years. The most faithful are closest to His side and have top positions. The first Lord's Prayer, *"Your will be done on earth, as it is in heaven"* is fulfilled; and so is the real Lord's Prayer, *"May all of them be one, just as You and I are one."*

Last Great Work of Holy Spirit

You are invited to be in on the last great work of the Holy Spirit. The day of Jesus' return will not come until His work in the Spirit is finished and the last person is saved. He has assured us of heaven. He is busy now completing His work through us so that He can return as promised. That promise should be our biggest reason for serving Him. Christ made it very plain He wants us to be prepared for His return. Our calling is to finish the race and win the prize. When all is ready, the Lord's promise on the day of His ascension will be fulfilled.

Spirit Power Action

Are you **prepared** to help Christ complete His work in the Spirit? Are you ready to meet the Lord? Or is there more you need to do? Review your progress and complete any work that needs to be done. You still have time left to bear fruit. When that glorious day comes for you to leave this world behind, you'll want to hear the Master's voice say, *"Well done, good and faithful servant; you have been faithful with a few things; I will put you in charge of many things; enter into the joy of the Lord!"* (Matthew 25:21).

The age of the Holy Spirit will soon end, the last person will be saved, and the Spirit's work will be accomplished on earth. Christ's return with all the saints will be a glorious day of triumph, the climax of human history, and the ultimate goal for which we strive. All those temporal sacrifices on earth to achieve eternal wealth of Spirit and outstanding places at Jesus' side in the kingdom will be worth it. Blood, sweat and tears will be replaced with glory, joy and peace. Wherever God is, we will be, never to be separated again!

"He who has initiated all these things declares, 'Yes, I am coming soon.' So be it; come, Lord Jesus!" (Revelation 22:20).

RAYS OF GOLD

Fourteen

FINAL WORDS FROM
C. S. LOVETT

"I have fought the good fight, I have finished the race, I have kept the faith. Now there is in store for me the crown of righteousness, which the Lord the righteous Judge, will award to me on that day—and not only to me, but also to all who have longed for His appearing" (2 Timothy 4:7-8).

When you graduate to heaven, you will rejoice and be glad! You have overcome the world, received your reward, and are ready to reign at the Lord's side—forever! My reward is to know I had a part in helping you prepare. That would be glory for me!

"Here I Am, Send Me!"

Do not sit by idly wondering,
What big work there is for you;
Success is an independent fellow,
He'll never come to you.

Consider Jesus' sweet promises,
Then give no thought or care;
If you want a place to work for Him,
You can find it anywhere.

Do not rob yourself by saying,
"There's nothing I can do,"
While hearts are yearning, begging,
And the Master calls for you.

Use the gifts He gave you freely,
"Go," is His tender plea;
Then be glad His call you answered,
"Here am I, send me. Send me."

Poem by C. S. Lovett (1917-2012)
© 2015 The Lovett Family Trust

APPENDIX

The Nicene Creed

The Early Church has given us the *Nicene Creed* to help distinguish between false teaching and true fundamentals of the Christian faith. The initial creed was adopted at the first Council of Nicaea in AD 325 to settle a controversy concerning the persons of the Trinity. It was intended to cover debated questions as to the divinity of Christ, and it introduced the word *homoousios* (Greek, "of the same substance") to correct the error of the *homoiousian* ("of like substance") party. To it were added several clauses against Arianism.

Filioque, combination of Latin words meaning "and from the Son," was added to the Nicene Creed by the Third Council of Toledo in 589: *Credo in Spiritum Sanctum qui ex patre filioque procedit* ("I believe in the Holy Spirit who proceeds from the Father and Son"). It refers to the doctrine of the procession of the Holy Spirit from the Father and the Son.

Today's Nicene Creed

Today's version of the Nicene Creed, the only Christian creed accepted as authoritative by the Roman Catholic, Eastern Orthodox, Anglican, and major Protestant churches, bears a resemblance to the original. Subsequent to the meeting in Nicaea, however, it underwent some changes. The creed below is used by Western churches in the Eucharistic liturgy and for both baptism and the Eucharist in Eastern churches. Its concise phrases have echoed Christian faith throughout the ages.

We believe in one God, the Father, almighty, maker of heaven and earth, of all things visible and invisible;

And in one Lord Jesus Christ, the only Son of God, begotten from the Father before all ages, light from light, true God from true God, begotten not made, of one substance (homoousios) *with the Father, through whom all things came into being, who for us men and for our salvation came down from heaven, and became flesh from the Holy Spirit and the Virgin Mary and became man, and was crucified for our sake under Pontius Pilate, and suffered and was buried, and rose again on the third day according to the Scriptures, and ascended into the heavens, and sits on the right hand of the Father, and will come again with glory to judge the living and the dead, of whose kingdom there will be no end;*

And in the Holy Spirit, the Lord and life-giver, who proceeds from the Father (and the Son [Filioque]), who with the Father and the Son is worshiped and glorified, who spoke through the prophets; and in one, holy, catholic and apostolic church. We confess one baptism for the remission of sins; we look forward to the resurrection of the dead and the life of the world to come. Amen.

We worship, praise, and pray to our Triune God the same way Jesus prayed to the Father. And it doesn't matter by what name we know Him—just so we call upon Him. How we worship Him is *unique* to every individual, and that's good. Who likes boring rituals of cookie-cutter faith? But we who believe the same God of the Trinity and *Nicene Creed* have the same faith, the same Jesus of our redemption, the same baptism of the Spirit, and the same God who created us all. Our spiritually challenged brains can't understand it all —especially the redemption—but we don't have to. All we need to know is that God loves us and we accept it by faith.

OTHER BOOKS BY C. S. LOVETT

Dealing with the Devil
Death: Graduation to Glory
Jesus Wants You Well
Lovett's Lights on 1st & 2nd Corinthians
Lovett's Lights on Acts
Lovett's Lights on Galatians - 2nd
    Thessalonians
Lovett's Lights on Hebrews
Lovett's Lights on John
Lovett's Lights on Revelation
Lovett's Lights on Romans
Lovett's Lights on Sermon on the Mount
Soul-Winning Made Easy
Unequally Yoked Wives
Witnessing Made Easy

Made in the USA
Las Vegas, NV
03 October 2021